New Vanguard • 65

British Napoleonic Artillery 1793–1815 (2)

Siege and Coastal Artillery

Chris Henry • Illustrated by Brian Delf

First published in Great Britain in 2003 by Osprey Publishing,
Midland House, West Way, Botley, Oxford OX2 0PH, UK
44-02 23rd St, Suite 219, Long Island City, NY 11101, USA
Email: info@ospreypublishing.com

© 2003 Osprey Publishing Ltd.

All rights reserved. Apart from any fair dealing for the purpose of private study, research, criticism or review, as permitted under the Copyright, Designs and Patents Act, 1988, no part of this publication may be reproduced, stored in a retrieval system, or transmitted in any form or by any means, electronic, electrical, chemical, mechanical, optical, photocopying, recording or otherwise, without the prior written permission of the copyright owner. Enquiries should be addressed to the Publishers.

Transferred to digital print on demand 2010

First published 2003
1st impression 2003

Printed and bound in Great Britain

A CIP catalogue record for this book is available from the British Library

ISBN: 978 1 84176 477 1

Editorial by Simone Drinkwater
Design by Melissa Orrom Swan
Index by Susan Williams
Originated by Grasmere Digital Imaging, Leeds, UK

Artist's note

Readers may care to note that the original paintings from which the colour plates in this book were prepared are available for private sale. All reproduction copyright whatsoever is retained by the Publishers. All enquiries should be addressed to:

Brian Delf
7 Burcot Park
Burcot
Abingdon
Oxon
OX14 3DH
UK

The Publishers regret that they can enter into no correspondence upon this matter.

FOR A CATALOGUE OF ALL BOOKS PUBLISHED BY
OSPREY MILITARY AND AVIATION PLEASE CONTACT:

Osprey Direct, c/o Random House Distribution Center,
400 Hahn Road, Westminster, MD 21157
Email: uscustomerservice@ospreypublishing.com

Osprey Direct, The Book Service Ltd, Distribution Centre,
Colchester Road, Frating Green, Colchester, Essex, CO7 7DW
Email: customerservice@ospreypublishing.com

www.ospreypublishing.com

BRITISH NAPOLEONIC ARTILLERY 1793–1815 (2) SIEGE AND COASTAL ARTILLERY

EQUIPMENT AND ORGANISATION

On a cold November night in 1783 at the Bull Inn, Shooter's Hill, a large group of artillerymen met Colonel Williams of the Royal Artillery to hear him regale them with tales from the siege of Gibraltar. Williams, a soldier of great renown, had just returned from the two-year battle against the Spanish in which he had been commander of the Rock's artillery. Nothing in the history of the Royal Artillery up to that time could compare with the siege of Gibraltar.

The great siege of Gibraltar of 1781–83 was for the most part an artillery duel punctuated by moments of activity and long periods of boredom. When the smoke had cleared the Royal Artillery had expended some 8,000 rounds and 716 barrels of powder. It was justifiably considered one of the greatest garrison defences the British Army had been involved in, and yet ten years later the Army was involved in an even greater conflict in which the taking and defending of towns relied heavily on a relatively small group of artillerymen and their equipment.

If one looks at a list of battles fought during the Napoleonic Wars an interesting fact becomes apparent: a number of these battles were fought as a result of sieges, such as the battle of Fuentes d'Onoro, fought in order to forestall Massena's resupply of Almeida in 1811. Fortified

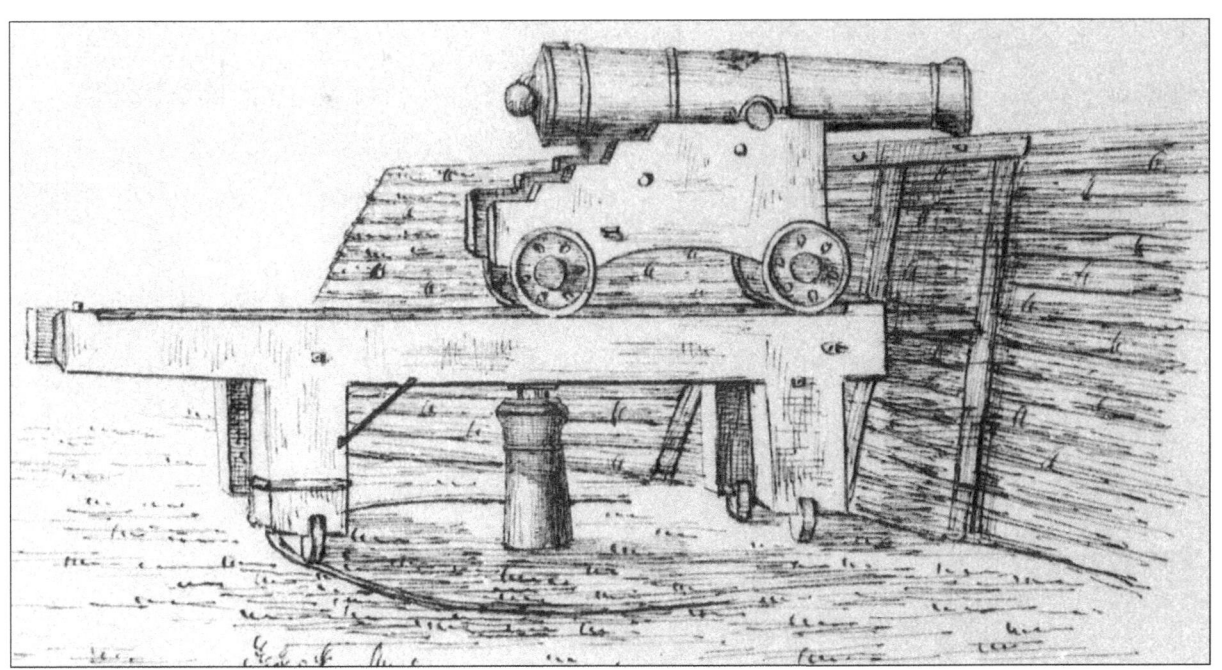

The traversing platform and garrison carriage. This was one form of mounting a coastal defence gun. Note that the central pivot is formed from an old gun barrel. The platform trucks ran on an iron ring or race. This drawing was made by a Royal Artillery cadet in a notebook of drawings from a course of instruction at the shop in the early nineteenth century. (Courtesy RAHT)

Also from a cadet notebook, an illustration of a 24-pounder siege gun and limber. The older small two-wheeled limber was still in use for this type of weapon, which would have been drawn mainly by oxen on campaign. (Courtesy RAHT)

strongpoints still dominated the transit routes of Europe and control of these places gave the military commander control of large areas of country out of all proportion to the forces required to maintain them. Sieges were a large part of military life. The time spent fighting field battles was less than the time spent besieging fortified towns. This process was not as pronounced as in the mid-18th century, but sieges were still an essential part of military campaigning in the Napoleonic period. The Peninsular War alone saw at least 17 major sieges and countless minor ones.

Defence of the coastline also became a very significant problem during the Napoleonic Wars. The French prepared to invade Britain on several different occasions and this forced the British government to revise its defences. The requirement to defend naval bases was critical because of Britain's reliance on naval power and a great deal of coastal artillery was concentrated around places like Plymouth and Portsmouth.

The key problem of Napoleonic coastal defence was the relatively short range of the smooth-bore guns then in use. This naturally dictated the nature of their emplacement. The guns had to be very close to the shoreline to be effective and therefore their siting was critical. In fact short range was also an issue in sieges since it obviously meant that a besieger's guns had to be placed near to the walls of the fortress or town. Elaborate defensive positions therefore had to be created to protect the guns from the fire of their opposite numbers on the walls of the besieged town.

Coastal guns and siege guns had one thing in common; they were guns of position. Their weight and size precluded easy movement so that once they were in their battery position they could only be redeployed with a great deal of effort. This lack of mobility made the siege train itself a ponderous beast requiring a colossal amount of effort to move it. This fact, tied to the atrocious roads and slow speed of draught animals, made a siege train very slow moving and a serious commitment on the part of the commander in time and money.

At sea heavy cast iron 32-, 24- and 18-pounder guns were the main armaments of the ships of the line, and these same weapons naturally found their way to land and became the main line of defence in places like Portsmouth, Plymouth and the Thames estuary. The link between land and sea armament was always close and the use of such coastal weapons was not hampered by the need to draw them by horses so their weight was often very great indeed.

Iron guns

The suppliers and users of ordnance often saw iron guns as the poor cousins of bronze pieces. This may have been for several reasons, but by the Napoleonic Wars iron guns were reliable and much cheaper to make than bronze. Their weight was their great drawback and although the bronze gun remained the most common on the battlefield, for coastal and siege work iron guns were far more widely used. They tended to be manufactured in similar calibres to naval guns such as 32-, 24-, 18- and 12-pounders. Even today many, many iron guns survive from this period.

The 32-pounder was the largest iron weapon that was regularly used for coast defence and naval service during the Napoleonic Wars. It was a reliable weapon, so much so that it remained in use long after this period. The gun was designed by Thomas Blomefield and was 9½ feet long and weighed 55½cwt. The design was very distinctive and all of the weapons were cast with a breaching loop at the back of the gun. Blomefield's design was far plainer than previous English guns, having fewer reinforces and an almost cylindrical appearance.

The 32-pounder was not normally used for siege work but two 24-pounders of similar design were. These were of 50cwt and 48cwt and 9½ and 9 feet respectively, although many other weights and lengths were available. Iron 24-pounders found their way to Spain and were heavily used there. During their first siege of Badajoz in 1811 the Anglo-Portuguese forces had as many as 13 24-pounders but not all of these were iron pieces.

Prior to Blomefield's designs some of the commonest forms of iron gun were those designed by John Armstrong. Armstrong worked as far back as the first quarter of the 18th century and he died in 1742, but his designs lingered on though modified by the proposals of Charles Frederick who was Surveyor of the Ordnance in 1760. The design originally envisaged by Armstrong was only slightly altered by Frederick's proposals but for our purposes the gun will be known as the Frederick

A gun and garrison carriage being transported by devil carriage. The devil carriage was a simple form of transport, which could be used to move many different artillery items. In this case it has the gun slung underneath it and the garrison carriage is placed on top upside down. There was another form of carriage called the drug which was used to transport barrels. (Courtesy RAHT)

A rear view of a heavy 18-pounder Blomefield gun on a reproduction common standing carriage. (Author's Collection)

pattern gun. Many guns of this period still exist and they were widely adopted for coastal defence. They were heavy and awkward to move and as a consequence were disliked by their detachments.

Iron 18-pounders also had a long service history in the artillery. There were many in existence at the beginning of the 18th century from at least five different types, but by the end of the century there were probably only two. Although the ranges of the various siege guns were similar the difference between the hitting power of a 24-pounder projectile and an 18-pounder was quite significant.

In general, commercial gun founders made iron guns for the Board of Ordnance. They sold their guns to the Board and were paid by weight. Commercial manufacturers were expected to produce their guns to a government design and there is a remarkable level of similarity between those designed by Blomefield for example, even when made by different foundries. One of the most prolific gun manufacturers was the Carron company of Falkirk, Scotland, which had something of a chequered history regarding reliability. The company supplied guns to the Board of Ordnance from as early as the 1760s and by the end of the period it had become a very large supplier. From the 1770s the company also became known for a new gun originally made for naval use. This short-barrelled low velocity weapon became known as the carronade because it was conceived and then manufactured at the Carron Iron Works.

Other companies supplying weapons during this period were Henckell and Company of Wandsworth, London, and the Low Moor Iron Company of Bradford. Many more companies were in existence and the Board called on these when demand was high.

The process by which bronze guns were made has been described in Osprey New Vanguard 60: *British Napoleonic Artillery 1793–1815 (1)* and the method of producing iron weapons was very similar. The main

The trunnion mark on an 18-pounder Blomefield gun. The G enclosed in a diamond could denote one of a number of manufacturers working for the Board of Ordnance; one possible company being Gordon and Stanley. (Author's Collection)

exception was that iron ore had to be smelted as part of the production process. This was done in a blast furnace with the iron then being run directly into the moulds.

The gun barrel was first made as a model in wood which was coated with a number of layers of clay and horsehair. Eventually the inner model was removed from the outer shell, which then formed the mould. A mould for the cascable section was made separately and then fixed to the bottom of the barrel mould. Molten iron was poured into the assembly and allowed to cool. The mould then had to be broken to get at the solid casting inside. This would then be placed on a horizontal lathe for the bore to be hollowed out. The casting was turned while a fixed cutting tool was forced into the muzzle end of the gun. It is thought that in Britain iron guns were first cast solid and bored out by a founder called Anthony Bacon in 1773. He worked in Merthyr Tydfil in Wales and contracted to the Board of Ordnance when it was seeking alternative suppliers after the failure of several Carron guns.

Gun design

At first glance it may seem that designing smoothbore guns is not a particularly complex business since, after all, the gun is just a tube into which the powder and projectile is placed. But many different factors have to be considered to get even a semblance of accuracy and control. Gun design was a gradual process and although major innovations, such as the carronade, did change aspects of gunnery, they were generally refinements on previous designs. It is important to understand that the army that fought the Napoleonic Wars had its roots in the 18th century. Gun designs and the infrastructure of gun supply were in place before the wars began. There was no definitive single system of artillery and therefore guns that were made long before the period were still widely used. It was not unusual to find several different designs of artillery piece in the same unit. A gun that was cast in the 1760s might easily find its way to the army in Spain or in the colonies 50 years later.

The mechanism for boring out a gun from solid. The gun revolves while the tool is forced into the muzzle of the piece on the left, as the barrel is rotated by the shaft at right. (Author's Collection)

The carronade is generally viewed as a naval weapon, which of course was how it started its life. It was a short-barrelled gun with a chamber and was intended to fire at short range with heavy shot but requiring a much smaller charge of powder. The design is normally attributed to either General Melville or Charles Gascoigne but it got its name from the Carron company, which was the first to manufacture the design. Carronades were used first by the Royal Navy in the War of American Independence. What is less well known is the fact that the carronade was also intended to be used in fortification and particularly in the Martello Towers which were to be a mainstay against Napoleon's intended invasion. In this respect 32-pounder and 24-pounder calibres were mentioned, although smaller calibres such as the 12-pounder also appear to have been considered. Although they were eventually viewed as inferior weapons for naval use, carronades continued long into the 19th century as flank defence weapons, and even though they had a shorter range than long guns they were considered to be a viable coast defence weapons.

Generally all of the dimensions of a gun were expressed in calibres or parts of a calibre. For example a 32-pounder gun with a calibre of 6.4 inches might be said to have a chase of a particular number of

A 24-pounder carronade on a block trail carriage. The block trail may have been in use for guns like this at the very end of the Napoleonic Wars. (Courtesy of the Trustees of the Royal Armouries)

calibres, say 10, which would mean that it measured 64 inches. There were many features of a gun that had a significant effect on its performance; the length and diameter of the trunnions, for example, and the position along the length of the gun that they were placed. The thickness of the metal at the breech or first reinforce was significant because it was thought that this part of the gun resisted the force of the charge explosion. In addition the muzzle swell was important because it had to cope with the change in air pressures when the projectile left the gun barrel. It was necessary for the gun to be as light as possible but strong enough to resist the shock of firing and heavy enough to have the minimum of recoil at the same time. Not until Thomas Blomefield created his designs in the 1790s was this balance really achieved. Blomefield was also attempting to standardise gun designs in the British army but had a mixed degree of success in this respect.

Proof

All guns were tested for soundness of construction. The process of examination and testing began with a thorough examination of the gun to check that the dimensions and tolerances were correct. These checks could also establish whether the bore was true or if any irregularities were present in it.

The guns were then fired with shot and powder to see if that exposed any further flaws. The test firing normally used much more powder for the charge than would be used for a standard gun firing, and sometimes the guns were double shotted as well. After this a water test was made by forcing water down the barrel to see if it leaked through the walls. This was often possible because the interior of the wall could be riddled with a strange honeycomb formation which was inherently weak, hence this phenomenon was known as honeycombing. The final test was to examine the walls again by means of the oldest test method of all, the eye. A mirror on a long pole was fed down the gun bore to see if any other problems had arisen as a result of the firing.

A view of the quarter sight scales on the side of a Blomefield design. These scales are marked on both the left and right side of the base ring for aiming the gun from point blank (when the gun was level) to three degrees. Each mark represents a quarter of a degree of elevation and these were aligned with a mark on the side of the muzzle of the gun. (Author's Collection)

BELOW A 13-inch bronze mortar cast in 1779 and of the exact pattern used at the beginning of the Napoleonic Wars. The mounting is modern. The cipher of the Master General of the Ordnance, George Viscount Townshend, is moulded above the vent. (Courtesy of the Trustees of the Royal Armouries)

Guns were not the only things to undergo proof; iron shells and shot were also subjected to tests to make sure they were fit for use. For shot this generally took the form of a visual examination followed by hammering all the way around the outside so that any loose sections fell off and flaws were exposed. Shells were tested in the same way and additionally they were placed in water with an empty fuse. The shell was immersed and air was forced by bellows into the shell. If no bubbles were seen coming from the surface of the shell it was considered to be proved.

Bronze guns

Large calibre bronze guns were still highly valued in this period. Bronze, an alloy of copper and tin, was strong enough to resist the forces exerted on it during firing and yet could be finely decorated. The mixture of the two metals was varied depending on the manufacturer, although it is interesting to note that the proportions of copper and tin in guns and howitzers varied to that of mortars. A typical mixture would be 87.1% copper, 6.65% tin, 0.15% zinc and 1% lead.

If we look at the sieges of the Peninsular War, the conflict in which a great deal of Britain's siege artillery was used, two main calibres of bronze guns stand out: the 24-pounder and the 18-pounder. Although heavier bronze guns, like the 42-pounder, were manufactured and recorded they did not often appear in action. If a heavier gun than the 24-pounder was required it would normally be in iron and would probably come from a ship.

A 10-inch bronze howitzer cast by John and Henry King in 1791. This was one of the heavier weapons used in sieges but it is not mounted on an original carriage. (Courtesy of the Trustees of the Royal Armouries)

A 24-pounder bronze gun was beautifully illustrated in C.W. Rudyerd's *Course of Artillery* of 1793. It was called the medium 24-pounder, was 8 feet long and weighed 41cwt. This gun is thought to have entered service in the 1750s and was still being used during the Napoleonic Wars. Similar guns were made at 5 feet 6 inches and 16cwt and 9 feet 6 inches and 52cwt. Thomas Blomefield was also involved in bronze gun designs and his 1790s design was 6 feet 3 inches long and weighed 24cwt. Various 18-pounders were similarly manufactured during the second half of the 18th century. A weapon of this calibre was also designed by Blomefield and became the 18-pounder of 5 feet 9 inches and 18cwt. It has been claimed that this type of gun was withdrawn after the failure of the siege of Badajoz in 1811 to be replaced by smaller howitzers such as the 5½-inch howitzer, which presumably was more mobile.

Theoretically during a siege a 24-pounder would be allocated 50 rounds of shot per day. The amount of powder used per round would vary from 2lb if the gun were to fire en ricochet or 8lb of powder were the full charge to be required. Even so an observation made by Major E.C. Cocks during the 1812 siege of Badajoz stated:

'A 100 shot per piece is the complement. Our powder is placed in a depot near the last trench from whence the battery magazines are fed, but enough is never brought into any magazine to occasion serious damage.'

Mortars and howitzers

The mortar was a high-angle low velocity weapon ranging from 2 inches to 13 inches in calibre in British service. Mortars had been in use as early as the 16th century and were considered to be ideal for attacking a town since they could lob a hollow gunpowder-packed projectile over the walls for it to explode in the town, causing damage to buildings and inflicting heavy casualties. Their destructive power was enormous and it is said that besieged armies would go to a lot of trouble to silence a mortar trained on a town. A mortar was normally cast with its trunnions at the end of the breech. It would then be mounted on a bed usually consisting of a solid wooden base with the mortar at a fixed elevation. In British service, varying the size of the powder charge altered the range of the shot. The powder chamber itself was normally smaller than the bore and considerable experimentation had gone on during the 18th century to find the most suitable shape of chamber for the best effects.

Mortars could be bronze or iron but traditionally they had been made of bronze – before 1792 most weapons were made of this material. The largest calibre was the 13-inch mortar. Initially this was a bronze weapon normally about 3 feet 7 inches in length and weighing some 25cwt. Two such weapons sit on top of the Beresford gate at Woolwich.

A very fine illustration of the 13-inch siege mortar being loaded onto a boat by means of sheer legs and block and tackle. From an early 19th-century cadet notebook drawn at Woolwich. (Courtesy RAHT)

They were made by William Bowen and Jan Verbruggen and their dimensions are almost identical. The sea service mortar was similar but was longer and more heavily reinforced at the breech. This type of mortar was 5 feet 3 inches in length and it weighed 80cwt. All of these bronze mortars had a tapered chamber normally altering in calibre by one inch along its length. By the end of the wars, iron mortars for land and sea service were in use. Iron 13-inch mortars were also very heavy, weighing just over 4 tons. The iron mortars were relatively short barrelled and fitted with trunnions.

It may seem odd in a book about siege and coastal artillery to include a section on sea service mortars but it is clear that they were intended to be used against coastal towns and therefore mention of them is relevant. Sea service mortars were heavier than land service mortars because they were expected to take a heavier charge. They were mounted on an oak bed which was pierced in the middle by an iron pintle. In this way the mortar could be traversed through 360 degrees inside a wooden enclosure on a ship's deck. Some bomb vessels, or bombs, as mortar-carrying ships were called, carried two 13-inch mortars while others carried a 10-inch and a 13-inch mortar. In 1804 the Royal Marine Artillery took over naval mortar duties from the Royal Artillery, whose job it had previously been to crew the mortars.

Prior to firing, the decks and the sails of the ship had to be doused with water and dampened screens were erected over the mortar vents to stop sparks escaping from these setting fire to the rigging. In order to keep the mortar in the right position the bed was wedged underneath to prevent it moving after the recoil. The officer in charge of the mortars would often try to get a vantage point in the rigging from where he could see the fall of the shell.

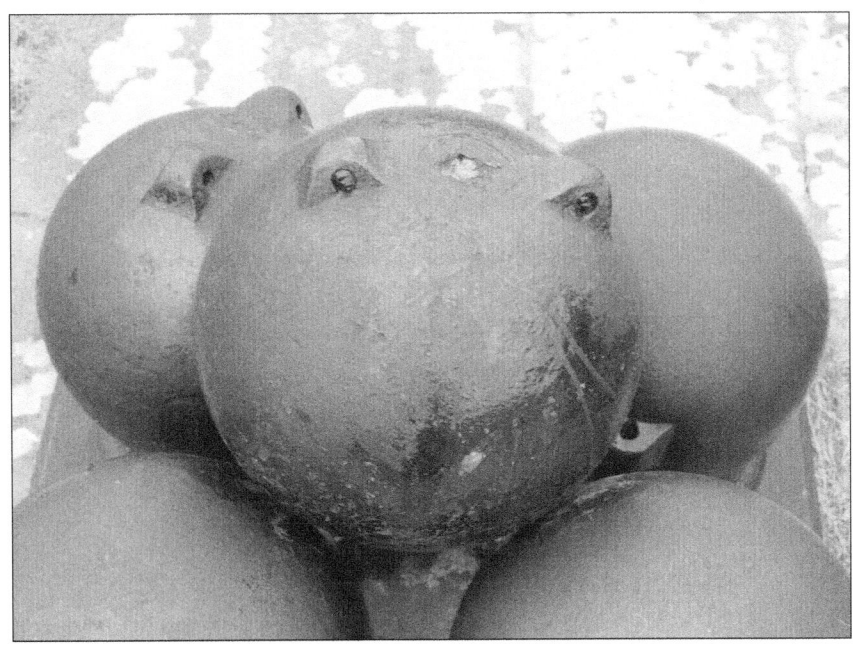

13-inch mortar shells. The two lugs and holes at the top of the shell were for lifting it via a winch. The metal of the shell wall was not uniform all the way around its circumference in the early part of the period and generally it was thicker opposite the fuse hole at the bottom of the shell. The fuse hole itself was conical with the diameter of the outer side being greater than the inner. The fuse itself was tapered and was hammered into the shell before firing. However, by the middle of the Napoleonic Wars experiments had been made to see if it was necessary to have this difference in thickness and it was found that shells with an equal wall thickness were more likely to burst into smaller pieces and be more effective. (Author's Collection)

There were two other calibres of iron land service mortar that merit some attention and they were the 10-inch and 8-inch weapons. Both calibres seem to have existed in two versions. One 10-inch weapon had a length of 2 feet 10.3 inches and the other a length 2 feet 3½ inches. They weighed 15½cwt and 16cwt respectively. The 8-inch mortar's two versions were proportional in size to the 10-inch weapons. All of these mortars were designed with a so-called Gomer chamber, named after its inventor, a Frenchman. This was effectively a tapered extension to the bore.

Smaller bronze mortars were widely used in siege work and the two smallest, the Coehorn and Royal mortars of 4⅖ inches and 5½ inches, were generally used in large groups.

How mortars were used was set out by R.W. Adye in 1802:

'The mortars are generally at first arranged in battery, adjoining the first gun batteries, or upon the prolongation of the capitals of the works; in which place they are certainly least exposed. Upon the establishment of the half parallels, batteries of howitzers may be formed on their extremities, to enfilade the branches of the covert-way; and upon the formation of the third parallel, batteries of howitzers and stone mortars may be formed to enfilade the flanks of the bastions, and annoy the besieged in the covert way.'

We can see then that because of its use as an anti-personnel weapon the mortar was highly valued and was moved from place to place to provide covering fire during a siege.

The mention of a stone mortar in Adye's text should be explained. This was a simple bronze mortar, which could be the size of a Coehorn but manufactured with thinner walls. As its name suggests it was made to fire stones. This was once thought to mean complete stone shot, but it is now meant to refers to showers of small stones, when fired at a high angle

A 10-inch mortar on its iron bed. The iron mortar weighed 17cwt and was one of the heavier versions of this mortar. (Author's Collection)

fell from a great height like deadly shrapnel pieces. Both howitzers and mortars had shorter ranges than guns. They were:

10-inch iron mortar	1,900 yards
10-inch brass mortar at 45 degrees	1,900 yards
8-inch brass mortar	1,600 yards
8-inch iron mortar	1,600 yards
5½-inch brass mortar	1,200 yards
4⅖-inch brass mortar	1,000 yards

A further weapon, which was neither a mortar nor a howitzer, was considered part of the siege train and that was the petard. The petard was really an explosive device for destroying the gates of a defended town. It appeared as an iron or bronze bell that was filled with gunpowder and was fixed to the enemy gates by means of hooks. The powder charge was about 10lb and the whole thing was fused. The fuse was lit by a length of quick match leading up to it. Using a petard was an extremely hazardous undertaking since the whole operation had to be carried out in front of the enemy and hence the expression 'hoist by one's own petard' has entered the English language as a euphemism for being caught by one's own device.

The bronze 8- and 10-inch howitzers were considered to be the main siege weapons of the day of this type. Normally a 10-inch howitzer was mounted on its travelling carriage but it is not clear how this was deployed in a siege battery. The 10-inch howitzer was a very hefty lump of metal weighing in at 25cwt approximately, compared with the 8-inch at a mere 13–14cwt. There were variations in size and weight of 8-inch howitzers between the mid-18th century and the 1820s but they tended to be around these weights, while the length of the barrel varied between 3 feet and 3 feet 6 inches.

Smaller iron howitzers were in development by 1800 and would seem that these were intended to be used for coastal defence. It is impossible to know if these were ever used but drawings exist for their carriages and cast examples certainly exist.

A 5½-inch or Royal mortar with the cipher of George III on the reinforce. The bed may be a Victorian addition since there are no iron fittings on the upper surface. (Courtesy of the Trustees of the Royal Armouries)

Rockets

The invention of the war rocket by William Congreve, the son of the great artillerist, was eventually to change the face of war. Congreve's system included rockets that ranged from 3lb in weight up to 300lb monsters. They were all stabilised by a long stick as in the modern day firework and could be fired from the ground or from a firing stand. Although the units using them were normally attached to the field artillery, war rockets were sometimes employed as siege weapons during the Napoleonic Wars. During the War of 1812, for example, they were credited with major destruction during the British attack on Washington and were also employed in the attack on Fort McHenry by HMS *Erebus*. However, it is difficult to say with certainty how effective the rockets were as siege weapons since their use in this role was rare – assessments tend to vary from nuisance value to a war-winning weapon.

Carriages and mountings

Surprisingly most heavy guns in the field still relied on a double bracket carriage construction method in this period. The 24-pounder was drawn almost exclusively on a double bracket system even though William Congreve's block trail design had been introduced for all British field guns early in the Napoleonic Wars. The travelling carriage for the 24-pounder was a relatively uncomplicated piece of technology that was formed of two cheeks, or horizontal members, connected together by transoms or short joining sections. The joined cheeks were mounted on an axletree bed which was then mounted on the iron axletree. The wheels were fixed to the axletree through their naves or hubs by lynch pins. They revolved round the axletree by means of tallow applied to the axles.

The difficulty in working out what colour, if any, field gun carriages were painted was discussed in Volume 1 and similarly we are not fully certain of the colour of siege gun carriages but some eyewitness accounts give us a strong lead. Take for instance the comments of Lieutenant John

Cooks of the 43rd Light Infantry at the attack on the convent of San Francisco during the siege of Ciudad Rodrigo in 1812:

> 'On the morning of the 14th, about five hundred French soldiers made a sortie from the city, and before they retired were very nearly succeeding in entering the batteries, where the battering cannon had been placed the night before. The twenty-four pounders were of iron, mounted like field guns on handsome carriages painted lead colour.'

It is not clear whether this image is intended to show a siege gun but the double bracket carriage is typical of heavy guns of the period. The team is composed of four horses but in wartime it would be six. (Author's Collection)

'Lead' was the name later used by the Victorians for the dark grey colour in which gun carriages were then definitely painted. This pigment consisted of lamp black, linseed oil and lead oxide in various proportions. However, in the Napoleonic period siege gun carriages were still sometimes drawn in cadet notebooks as if they were unpainted and the plates in this book therefore show guns both painted and unpainted to illustrate this.

The commonest form of gun carriage for fixed defences was the common standing carriage, but this was not the only form designed for fortification. The common standing carriage was a simple affair of two side brackets connected by transoms at front and rear and a simple wooden axletree front and rear, where the axles were wooden protrusions with an iron band around the extreme end of the stub. The trucks or wheels were of cast iron (at sea they were wood to reduce the amount of damage done to the ships' decks when the guns recoiled). The wheels were held on to the carriage by an iron lynch pin through the wooden axletree. The carriage itself was held together by iron bolts passing through the axle and body at various places. The carriages had a curious stepped design at the rear that enabled a handspike to gain purchase on the carriage so that the gun could be easily elevated.

Although the gun itself was a relatively unchanged weapon, the traversing mounting used in fixed defences went through a number of alterations during this period of warfare. The traversing mounting could be one of a number of designs which varied in detail. One type was a rectangle of wood mounted on a high platform to allow the gun to fire over the defensive wall. The rectangle attached to a fixed pivot at one end and followed a described arc at the other. A common standing carriage was mounted on the two longest sides of the rectangle. The gun, therefore, could recoil along the top of the rectangle and it could be moved from side to side to traverse. Runners were attached to the top surfaces of the long sides of the rectangle to ensure that the gun ran along the axis of the carriage when it recoiled. A sketch of this type of carriage was made in the Scilly Isles in 1793.

There is also plenty of pictorial evidence to suggest that other traversing platforms pivoted about the centre or front. This includes watercolour drawings that are part of the Shuttleworth collection of 1819 held at the Royal Artillery Library in Woolwich, but it is very likely that this type of design existed before this date. The images show the common garrison carriage mounted on a rectangle of timber baulks all supported on four short legs. The four short legs each have a truck, or wheel, mounted on their ends and these run along a race or metal track fitted to the ground. In the centre of these legs is a pivot, which extends into what appears to be the muzzle of an old cannon about which the platform rotates. The platform is angled so that the gun carriage recoils up the slope.

A traversing carriage of cast iron was certainly in existence from 1810, when it was mentioned by the Board of Ordnance, but it may not have been used until after the wars.

All of the platform designs appear to be slightly different in some way and it may be they were adapted to the fortification or the country in which they were mounted. It is, however, clear that the artillerymen of the day attempted to regulate the size and construction of these mountings but it seems that this was only achieved after this period.

Before the Napoleonic period howitzer carriages had traditionally been of a double bracket construction with three transoms and short reinforced cheeks. The length of the cheeks was around 101 inches, making the carriage appear much shorter and stubbier than the gun

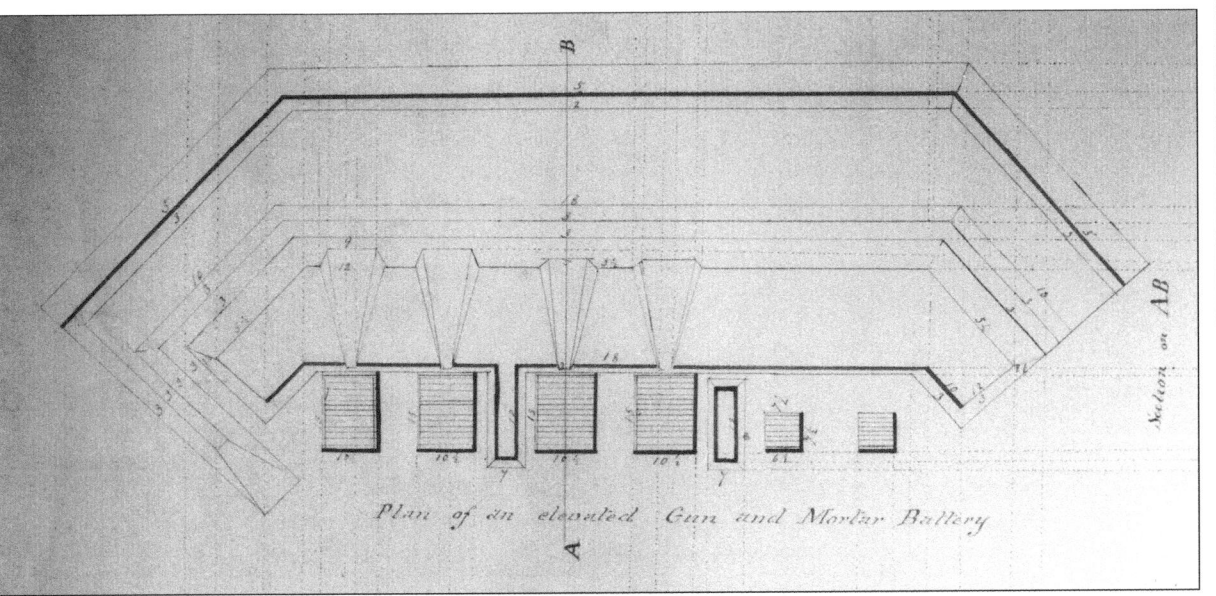

A gun position seen in plan form. The wooden platform was essential in siege work since it gave a stable platform for the gun to fire on. The continuous recoil of the guns would soon churn up the position and cause grave difficulties with the guns if the whole position were not carefully prepared. The square blocks between each pair of guns are the traverses, embankments intended to protect each pair from flanking fire. The two smaller platforms are for mortars. (Author's Collection)

A traversing gun position with a modern reproduction of the traversing platform. This centre pivot mount uses two races or metal tracks. The circular one on the raised mount is the central pivot whereas the outer race is semicircular and describes the arc of traverse of the gun. (Author's Collection)

carriages of the period. There are some drawings that suggest that some howitzers were mounted on Congreve's new design, but none of these show the 8- or 10-inch howitzers. It is likely that these heavier weapons were not mounted on the new carriages and remained on the old double bracket design as illustrated by Rudyerd in the 1790s. This version of the design relied on the limber having much smaller wheels and a very long pintle on which the trail was hooked.

Standing carriages are known to have been designed for the 8- and 10-inch howitzers but their designs have been lost to obscurity.

Mortars were normally mounted on beds. These were hollowed out blocks of wood placed on the ground and designed to take the shock of firing. The larger beds for the 13-inch and 10-inch mortars were fitted with extensive iron work in the form of lifting rings, traversing lugs, cap squares and reinforcing bands. The smaller beds were just a simple block of wood. Cast iron mortar beds came into use in about 1790 and were made as relatively simple single castings with the trunnion holes centred in the middle of the bed. Although there was generally no provision for changing the elevation of the piece, this type of mortar bed could be complemented by a wooden bolster, which was a wedge placed under the chase of the mortar and designed to support it. Mortars were generally carried on a wagon or sling cart and manhandled into position. This must have been an extremely onerous exercise when using the 13-inch land service mortar, even though the officers and men were well trained to cope with the process.

Transport

Clearly the horse was the most common draught animal during this period, but oxen were also widely used in war especially during the Peninsular campaign. Movement of guns and equipment could be carried out in many different ways according to circumstances and it was the artillerists' duty to learn the best ways of handling heavy weights of one ton or more. As with most engineering exercises this was achieved by manpower and winches and pulleys. Most of the training for this work was done at the Royal Military Repository at Woolwich and guns were fired on Woolwich Common and Shooter's Hill.

Gunners often dismounted guns so that their barrels and carriages could be stored or transported separately and therefore it was important that they were familiar with the tools of the trade such as handspikes, sheers, gyns and all the other lifting equipment they would need. The artillery gyn was a tripod, which could be constructed over a gun carriage so that a block and tackle was positioned over the centre of balance of the gun. It was then winched up out of its position on the carriage.

The gunners all learned what were known as repository exercises. These were exercises designed to get the men to learn all of the different ways of lifting, hauling and positioning gun barrels and carriages. Parbuckling was one such exercise in which the gunners learned to roll a barrel in order to move it to where it was required. Guns could be rolled up a slope by levering the gun onto wooden skids and passing a rope underneath the breech and chase. The rope would then be attached firmly to a hardpoint at the top of the slope and the end of the rope passing under the gun would then be led up the slope to where the gunners were standing at the top. The gunners would then pull on the rope to produce a rolling motion. By using mechanical advantage in this way very heavy weights could be moved about with a modest number of men.

There were also different types of carriages designed to move the guns apart from the travelling carriage. The sling cart and sling wagon were used for moving heavy guns. The sling cart was two wheeled and could move guns, mortars and howitzers up to 65cwt in weight. The wheels were very large at around seven feet in diameter. The barrel was slung underneath the cart not far from the ground. There was also a cart, known as a devil cart, which performed much the same function. The sling wagon was a much larger vehicle, of which there were several

A plain stone embrasure for a garrison gun mounting. (Author's Collection)

Detail of an iron garrison carriage truck. 'Truck' was the general term for the smaller type of wheel that was fitted to garrison carriages. These were normally about 19 inches in diameter. The lynch pin was of cast iron and fitted into a hole made in the axle. (Author's Collection)

versions that could lift up to 20 tons. It was formed by a wooden frame that was directly attached to the pintle of the early bolster limber. The four-wheeled carriage had a windlass fitted over the axletree that could winch the barrel into position. The barrel was supported under the trunnions by metal thimbles and a 6-inch rope. The barrel was normally raised so that the muzzle faced to the rear and the breech was lashed to the upper frame. The gun carriage could be mounted on the upper side of the wagon. A further type of gun transport was the drug, which was a carriage mounted on trucks used for moving heavy guns in positions where the size of the platform would be inconvenient. The heaviest could be drawn by four horses abreast whilst the smaller versions were equipped to be pulled by men.

Ammunition and equipment

Most of the different types of ammunition that were available to field artillery were available to siege and coastal artillery. Round shot, common shell, canister, spherical case, carcass and grape (Volume 1 has a full description of these different types) were all allocated to siege and coastal batteries.

Common shell was used for harassing fire during sieges and was considered to be excellent for disrupting defensive fire from fortifications. This was normally only fired from a mortar or howitzer and was a hollow sphere filled with a gunpowder charge. By the end of the period the shell had thinner walls the same thickness all the way around. The fuse, ignited by the discharge of the gun, had a central channel drilled through it in which a special composition burned. Before firing it was cut to a certain length corresponding to the desired range and time of burning and hammered into the top of the shell by a mallet. When it arrived over the target the fuse exploded the main charge, breaking open the metal outer casing and forcing flying fragments in all directions.

The artillery gyn and its component parts. (Courtesy RAHT)

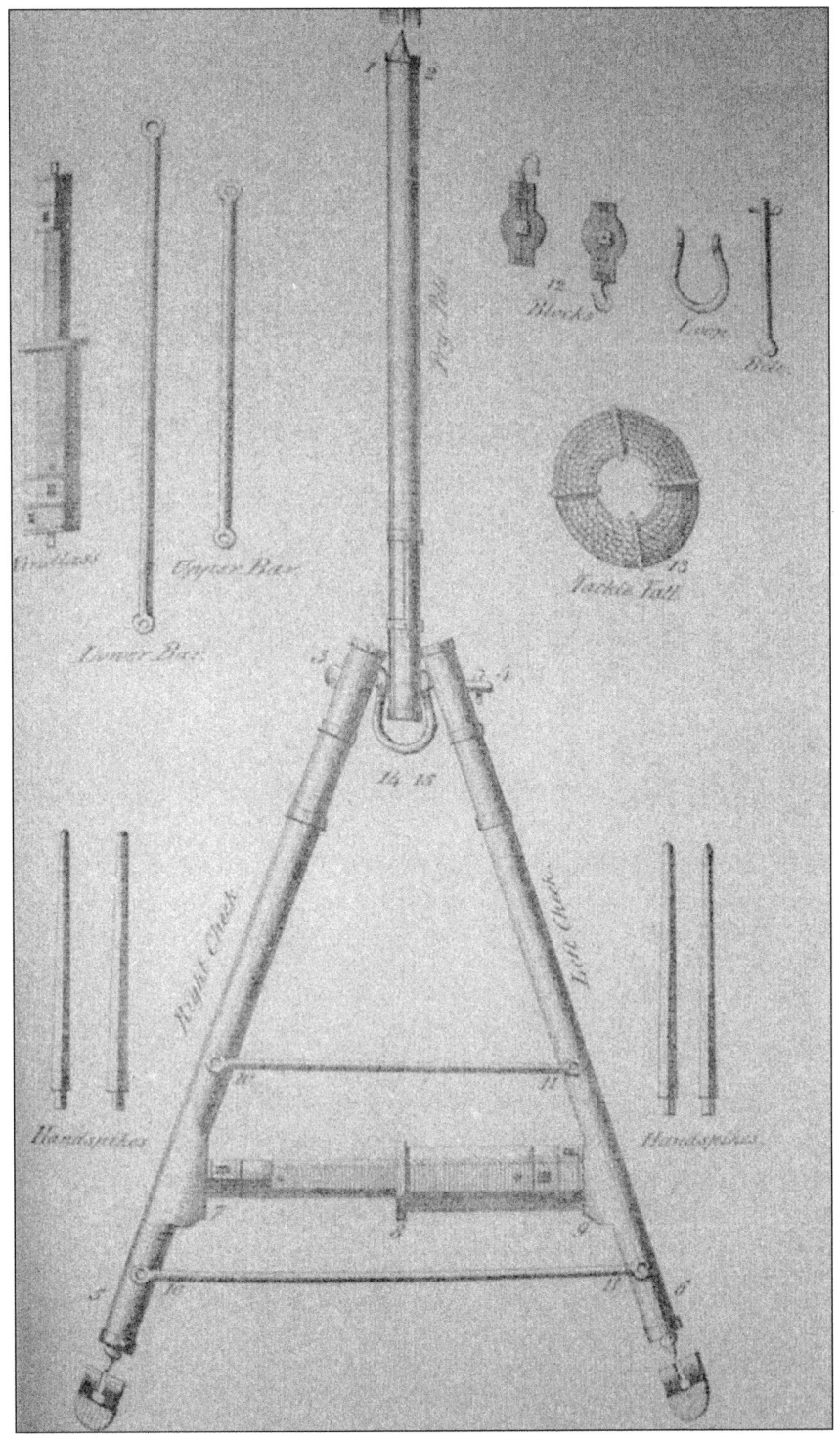

The significance of fire as a weapon against ships and wooden buildings meant that incendiaries were particularly favoured, especially by coastal batteries. Red hot shot was a particularly devastating weapon against wooden ships. In order to fire red hot shot the guns needed a brazier to heat the projectile and it took about three-quarters of an hour

A sling wagon and 8-inch mortar. This early 19th-century notebook illustration demonstrates the method of placing a mortar on top of the sling wagon by using luff tackle and skids. The upper image shows a method of dismounting a gun by means of boxes and a lever. The carriage appears to be a sea service type by its wooden trucks and may have been an obsolete item used for training cadets. This image demonstrates the clear flouting of Health and Safety rules in the 19th century! (Courtesy RAHT)

to get the shot hot enough. In addition, for safety the powder had to be put in strong flannel bags, sometimes doubled up. The charge was rammed home and a dry wad was rammed after it. After this a wet wad was rammed down the barrel before the shot was loaded. The wet wad was designed to stop the hot shot from detonating the firing charge prematurely. Normally in a garrison battery the gun would bc in an elevated position and have to be depressed to aim at its target and therefore another wad would finally be rammed home to hold the shot in place. Once all this was done the gunners would have time to aim and fire the gun before there was any danger of the piece discharging by itself.

Spherical case was considered to be the new wonder weapon of the wars. Invented by Henry Shrapnel it consisted of a hollow iron shell filled with lead musket balls and bursting powder. The shell was fired and the fuse set in train an explosion inside the shell, which scattered lead shot down onto the target. These shells were probably of more use to a besieged army than to besiegers because they could play along the attacking trenches.

Tools for siege guns were similar to those for field guns and consisted of ladles, sponges, rammers, trail spikes, portfires, linstocks and others. The main difference between these tools was their size. With a very large gun, such as a 32-pounder, the bore would be about 7 inches in diameter.

Detail of the cap squares and trunnion holes. There were two positions on the travelling carriage as is shown here. The front position was for firing while the rear position was for travelling. This system was used on carriages of the double bracket type. (Courtesy of the Trustees of the Royal Armouries)

Therefore the rammer head and sponge head had to be about the same size. A wooden head on the end of a pole about eight to nine feet long is an unwieldy instrument and not surprisingly it took more time and more men to load and fire one of the great guns. It was common for siege and coastal guns to dispense with the rammer-sponge combination and have each as a separate side arm, but some illustrations still show the guns with combination tools.

Training and personnel

As has been mentioned the home of the Royal Artillery was Woolwich and it was here that gunners were trained to deal with all types of siege weapon. Officers were trained at the Royal Military Academy on the river until 1805 when they moved to the Shop, as it was known, on Shooter's Hill, now a Ministry of Defence establishment.

As has been described in the companion volume on field artillery, all artillery crews were known as detachments. The main unit for siege artillery was the company and detachments of men were told off to serve the guns. There is some contradictory evidence as to how this was done but both Cavalié Mercer and Adye mention that gunners on field guns were numbered from 7 upwards for those men actually serving the gun. Mercer states that for garrison guns the numbering went from 1 upwards – 1 sponges, 2 loads, etc. – and that for field guns when there were drag ropes the numbers also began at 1, but then the first six were drag-rope men and those serving the gun began at 7. Coastal artillery units were more complex than their field cousins because they would have to adapt the artillery company to serve whatever guns were available to them to defend the positions they were allocated.

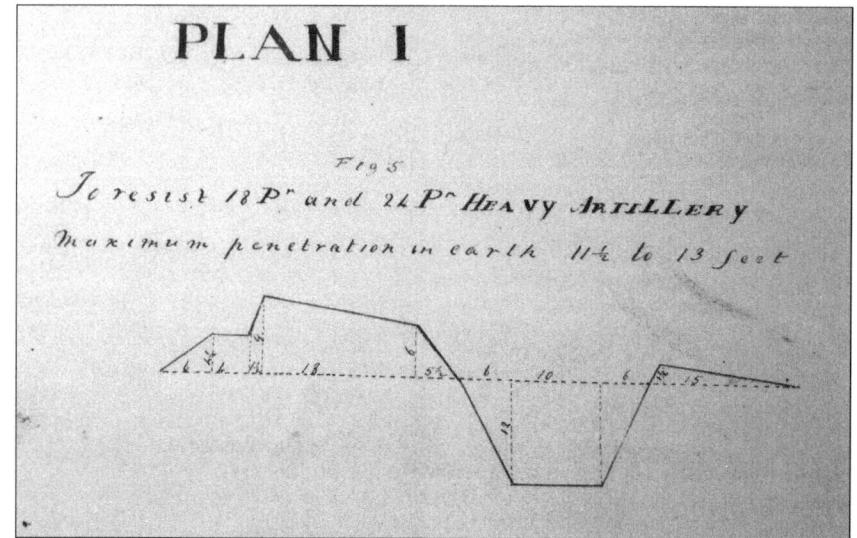

Elevation of an earthwork designed to resist fire from 18- and 24-pounder guns. The image is a 19th-century drawing by a gentleman cadet of the Royal Engineers which was intended to show various field engineering works to be constructed for siege batteries. (Author's Collection)

With a large siege gun, such as a 24-pounder, the detachment normally consisted of 15 men. However, if the gun was not to be moved, the detachment was of nine men. Nevertheless, most theorists advocated that guns should practice with smaller detachments because it was likely that men would be incapacitated or killed in action, thus reducing the numbers. It was considered that a 24-pounder siege gun could be fired by only three men if need be, though practical experience has shown the author that with a large-bore gun it always takes more than one man to sponge and ram and often it takes three.

In a siege gun with a full detachment the NCO commanded the gun. According to Adye, with nine men present, 1 sponged the gun and was positioned outside the right wheel and muzzle when viewed from the rear of the gun; 2 loaded and rammed (helped by 1) and was positioned outside the left wheel; 7 served the vent from clear of the right wheel; 8 fired from clear of the left wheel, like 7 in line with the vent; 3 and 5 ran the gun up. 4 ran up and elevated the rest of the detachment. 1 to the rear supplied ammunition.

The main difference between field and heavy gun drill seems to have been that the gunners stood to the outside of the wheels when working the gun. The drill described above was the theoretical ideal and it is clear that soldiers diverted from it on occasion. In a battery with eight men 1 sponged, 2 loaded, 3 and 4 ran the gun up and elevated the barrel, 5 served the vent and helped run the gun up as well as traversing and priming the gun, 6 ran up, traversed and fired, 7 brought the cartridges and 8 pointed and commanded.

It was quite common especially in the West Indies to parcel groups of men out to serve the guns at separate locations so that, for example, on Dominica in 1805 there were several defensive strongpoints that required a gun crew: Fort Cabril, Roseau and Scott's Head. All had between five and 27 guns as armament. There was only one officer and 41 gunners for the whole island and so they were split into small groups and sent off to the various outposts. Since each gun required at least seven men to operate it West Indian gunners and soldiers of the 46th Foot made up the shortfall.

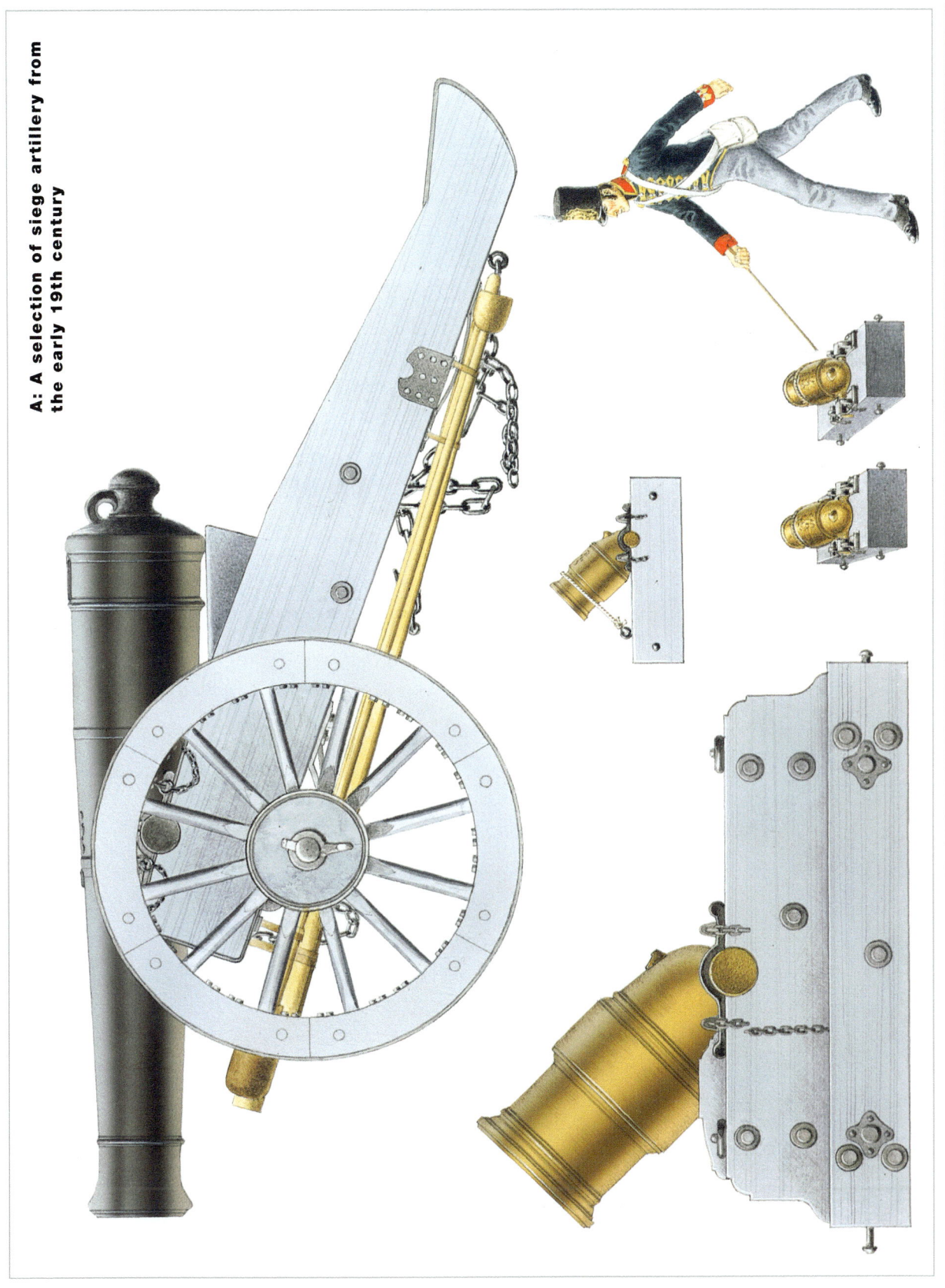

B: Part of a battery at the siege of Badajoz in 1811

C: Different natures of siege ordnance

D: SEA SERVICE MORTARS

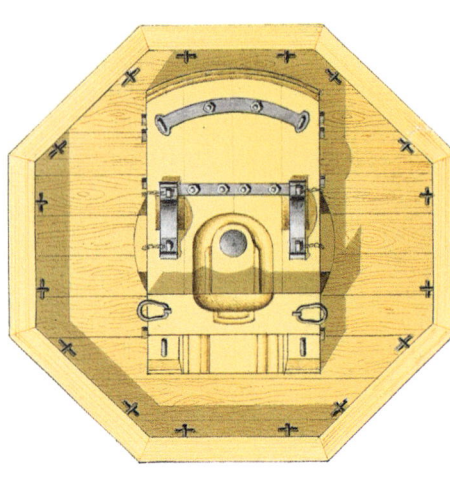

KEY

1 House
2 Bed
3 Cap square
4 Iron dolphins
5 Muzzle ring
6 Shell hoist
7 Shell lockers
8 13-inch mortar shell
9 Traversing lug
10 13-inch mortar shell
11 Bronze dolphins
12 Chase
13 Approximate position of the end of the chamber
14 Mortar pit support beam
15 Trunnion side view
16 Eyebolt key securing chain
17 Bolster
18 Pintle
19 Transverse bolt with ring
20 Lashing bolts
21 Vent
22 Loop bolt
23 Riveting plate
24 Cap square
25 Combined bolster and bed
26 Shell passage

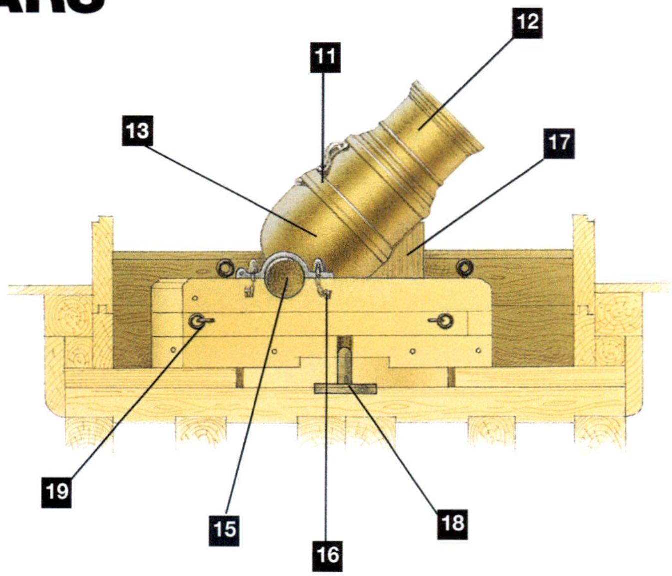

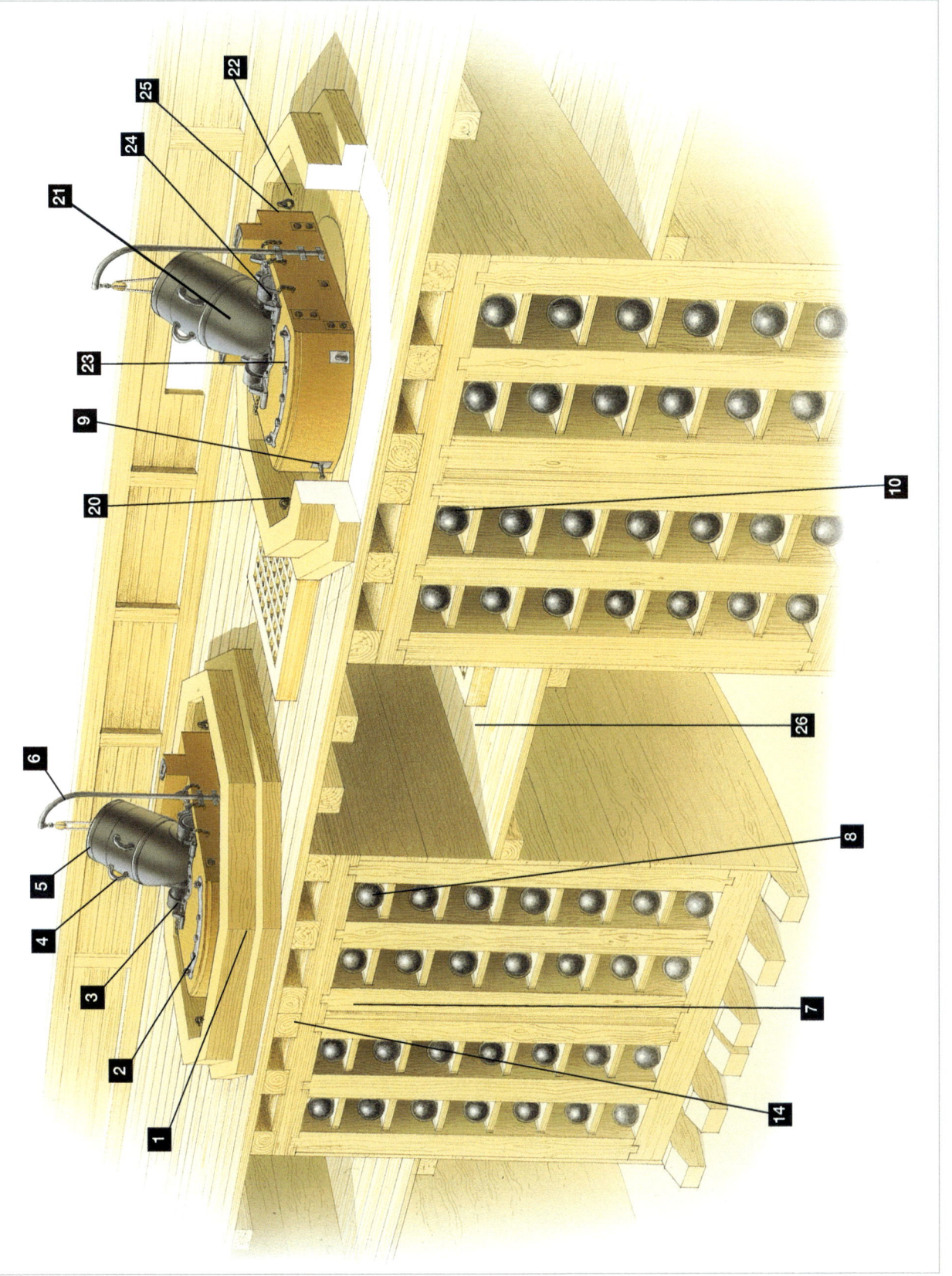

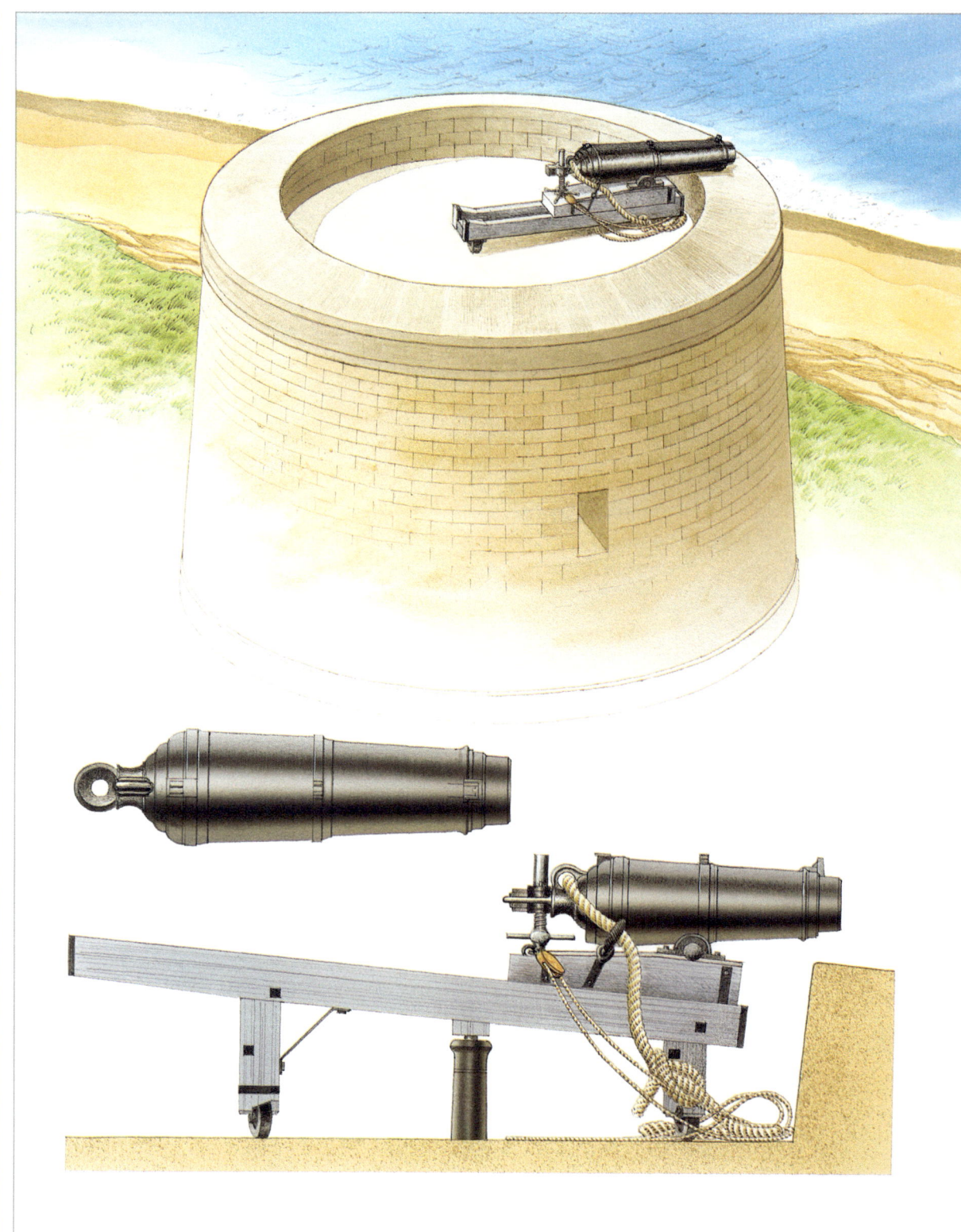

E: The carronade in coastal use

F: Coastal defence guns in a battery position

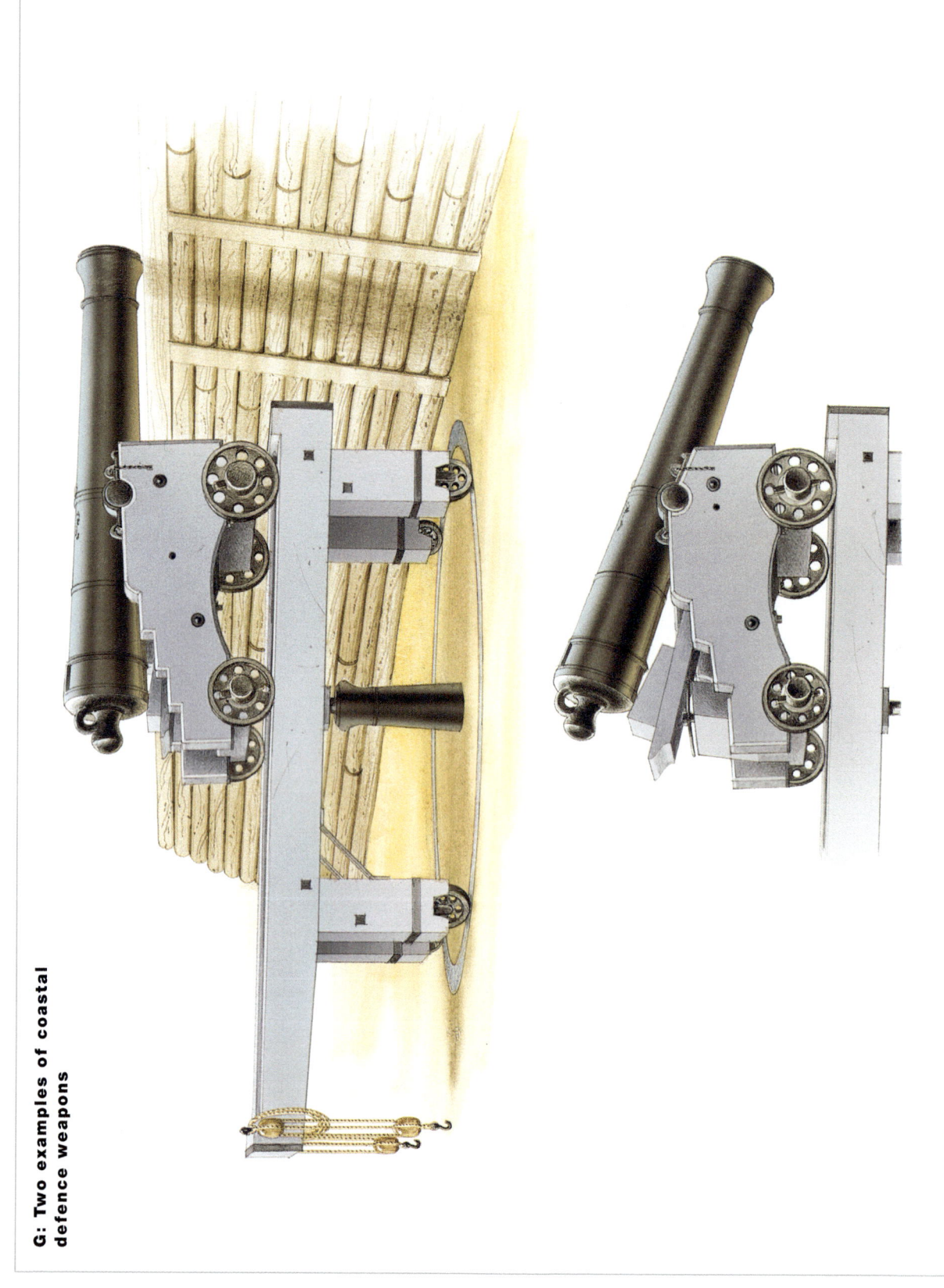

G: Two examples of coastal defence weapons

The early home of the gunners and Royal engineers was the Royal Military Academy at Woolwich. This 18th-century drawing shows gun barrels and shot lying around in abundance. (Courtesy RAHT)

Draught animals

Many theorists who wrote on artillery in the mid-18th century were still studied during the Napoleonic period and one such author, Le Blond, wrote of the exact compliment of horses that should accompany an artillery train. Taking a brigade of four 24-pounders as an example, he estimated that 48 horses would be needed to pull the guns, one team of eight to pull the spare carriages, one team of four to pull the wagon of 300 tools, making 132 horses in all. When it is considered that a full siege train might contain six or eight such units one realises that around 1,000 horses might well be required. Quite clearly this could be a logistical nightmare when all of those horses required watering and feeding with fodder that might well have to be carried with them.

In Spain, bullocks were relied on quite heavily to do this job. They were more durable and required less careful management and as a bonus could readily be eaten when times were hard. The disadvantage, according to the Duke of Wellington, was that a bullock cannot move much faster than about 12 miles a day. They were also in short supply in the Peninsula and this seriously affected Wellington's ability to bring up ammunition and supplies, thus hampering his siege operations.

Mules, too, were widely used, both individually and in teams. Again, not only were the animals in short supply but they needed wheat and rye that had to be foraged from the surrounding area or transported with them. This was a real problem. Wellington stated that he lost 1,500 mules during the first phase of the Peninsula campaign. Officers of the artillery were sent to Gibraltar to try to purchase horses from North Africa to feed the shortfall.

Coastal defence

As was mentioned at the beginning of this book the defence of Gibraltar was one of the greatest sieges in the 18th century. Gibraltar was an essential naval base and also controlled access to the Mediterranean.

An 8-inch iron mortar on an iron bed. This type of cast iron bed is thought to have been invented by Thomas Blomefield and this particular mortar dates to about 1800. The weapon weighs 8cwt and was superseded by a longer heavier version in the 1820s. (Courtesy of the Trustees of the Royal Armouries)

The redoubtable Major E.C. Cocks was present at Gibraltar in 1809–10. He recorded the number of guns on the island during the period, which came to 627, a figure which demonstrates the high priority that Britain gave to defending the Rock.

The breakdown was as follows:

IRON		BRONZE	
42-pounders	27	26-pounders	2
32-pounders	88	18-pounders	2
26-pounders	6	12-pounders	23
24-pounders	230	6-pounders	14
18-pounders	52	3-pounders	2
12-pounders	50	10-pounder Irish howitzers	17
6-pounders	10	8-pounders	21
4-pounders	4	6½-pounder howitzers	4
68-pounder carronades	15	10-pounder Irish mortars	1
24-pounder carronades	21	5½-pounder mortars	1
13-pounder Irish mortars	26	1⅔ mortars	1
10-pounders	6		
8-pounders	1		

This was a very mixed bag indeed and it seems to have included foreign guns and those either used in Ireland or manufactured there.

There were many common factors between coastal defence artillery and naval gunnery. When attacking ships the coastal gun often had the advantage of height and the cover of a gun emplacement. Coastal guns would normally be arranged behind a parapet or epaulment. This could have embrasures or equally the gun could just fire over the top. It was suggested that they should have about 18 feet between each gun

A bronze 8-inch mortar by John and Henry King cast at Woolwich Arsenal in 1805. The bed is a large cast iron square which was not a service platform and may have been custom made for saluting batteries. (Courtesy of the Trustees of the Royal Armouries)

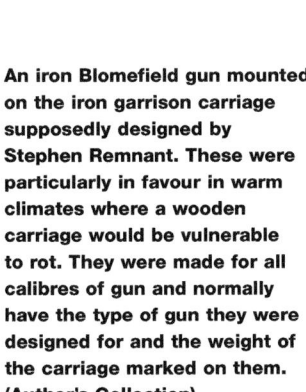

An iron Blomefield gun mounted on the iron garrison carriage supposedly designed by Stephen Remnant. These were particularly in favour in warm climates where a wooden carriage would be vulnerable to rot. They were made for all calibres of gun and normally have the type of gun they were designed for and the weight of the carriage marked on them. (Author's Collection)

especially if mounted on traversing carriages. In each case the lower edge of the gun barrel was normally about six inches above the defensive work when trained horizontally. According to the great French artillerist Gribeauval, coastal guns could be used to fire a ricochet shot at enemy ships when they were placed about 45 to 50 feet above sea level. The gun position was recommended to have the earth cut in steps in front of it so that the return fire would be broken up or misdirected. Again smaller pieces could be placed further up on cliff tops which would be able to fire on the fighting tops of attacking ships. It was estimated that a battery of four or five guns was enough to match a first-rate man-of-war. Whether this was really the case depends on which campaign one looks at during this period.

During the West Indian campaigns of the 1790s garrison artillery was heavily engaged against indigenous revolts and the fire of French revolutionary fervour sweeping through the islands. The campaigns are a good example of the value attributed to coastal fortifications and gunnery. In 1795–96 there were eight companies of Royal Artillery based

35

in the islands as follows: three companies on Martinique, one company on Jamaica, one company on Barbados, one company on St Kitts, and two companies distributed among the smaller islands along with three companies of Royal Irish Artillery. Possession of various islands was regularly contested by the French and Spanish and garrison gunners were constantly engaged with soldiers or ships trying to control the islands.

GUNS IN ACTION

The siege was, by its very nature, a long drawn out process. From the point of the attacking forces, time taken to establish which was the weakest point of the fortification was never wasted. Possibly the greatest proponent of the siege in the Napoleonic Wars on the British side was Major-General Sir Alexander Dickson. He was present at the siege of Valletta in 1800, the assaults on Buenos Aires in 1806–07, and, from 1811, became Wellington's artillery commander in the Peninsula. Dickson was involved in every aspect of artillery use and has left us an interesting series of memoirs which shed some light on the use of siege artillery. For example, in a letter to General McLeod in 1811 on the siege of Badajoz Dickson wrote that:

'I think 17 or 18 24-pounders were rendered hors de combat, two of which only were by the enemies' fire and the remainder by drooping at the muzzle and unbushing.'

The term 'unbushing' refers to the tendency of guns to wear away at the vent because of the passage of high velocity gas on firing. If left unrepaired this would greatly reduce the power of the gun. By the Napoleonic period it was possible to drill the vent of a gun and fit a bush

A 24-pounder bronze gun on a heavy siege carriage. This gun was one of a number of bronze French guns captured at Cherbourg and was cast in 1762. It is mounted on a block trail siege carriage of the mid-19th century which was not issued to the siege artillery until after the Napoleonic period. No original large wooden gun carriages have survived and this gives an impression of the size and scale of the weapon. (Courtesy of the Trustees of the Royal Armouries)

or copper vent into the widened hole, thus fixing the problem. In time this bush would wear loose and come out, leaving the gun 'unbushed' and in need of further repair.

An interesting comparison can be made between the performance of iron and bronze guns under siege conditions where each was expected to fire at least 50 rounds a day. A common failure of bronze guns was, as Dickson noted, their tendency to overheat and 'droop'. This meant that the barrel curved downwards inevitably affecting the accuracy of firing and endangering the crew. This is confirmed by Major Cocks, who was present at the siege in 1811.

Normally a town had to be surrounded if it was to be besieged and once this was done a series of complex field works was begun to protect the besiegers and, more importantly, their guns. Once the siege had started, the guns would be prime targets because they would effect a breach in the walls bringing about the destruction of the garrison. An initial trench would be dug parallel to the wall to be attacked (this trench would be called the first parallel) and guns set up in it or in batteries nearby. Further trenches called saps would then be dug toward the walls to bring the attacking troops within range for an assault while the guns continued their dual roles of destroying the walls and counteracting the artillery within the fort. The saps might be linked by further parallels as they got closer to the defences and some guns be brought forward to be sited in these.

More detail on the conduct of sieges is given in many other works on Napoleonic warfare and so this section will deal with the guns themselves. The Royal Engineers were responsible for deciding where the weaker points of the defence were. Once this was established the gunners then began to set up their batteries in order to exploit this weakness. Contemporary sources stated that there should be at least two kinds of batteries: the enfilading batteries and the breaching batteries.

A longitudinal view of a rectangular gun battery for artillery at a siege. (Author's Collection)

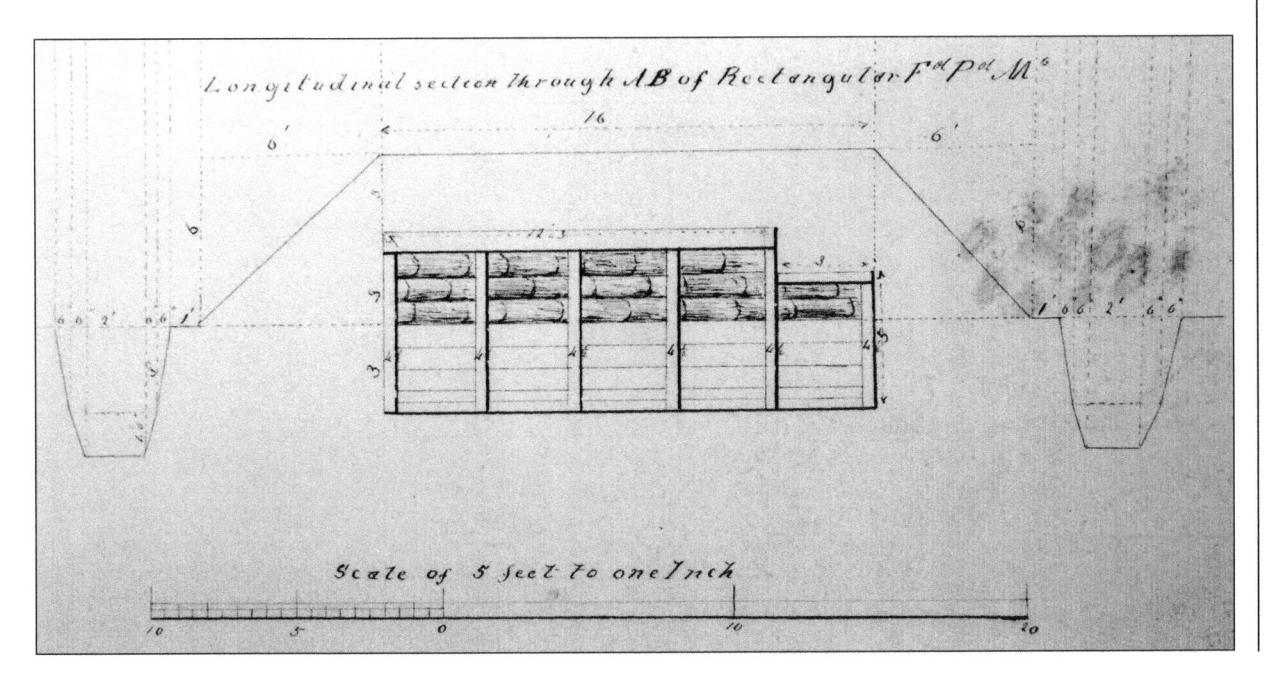

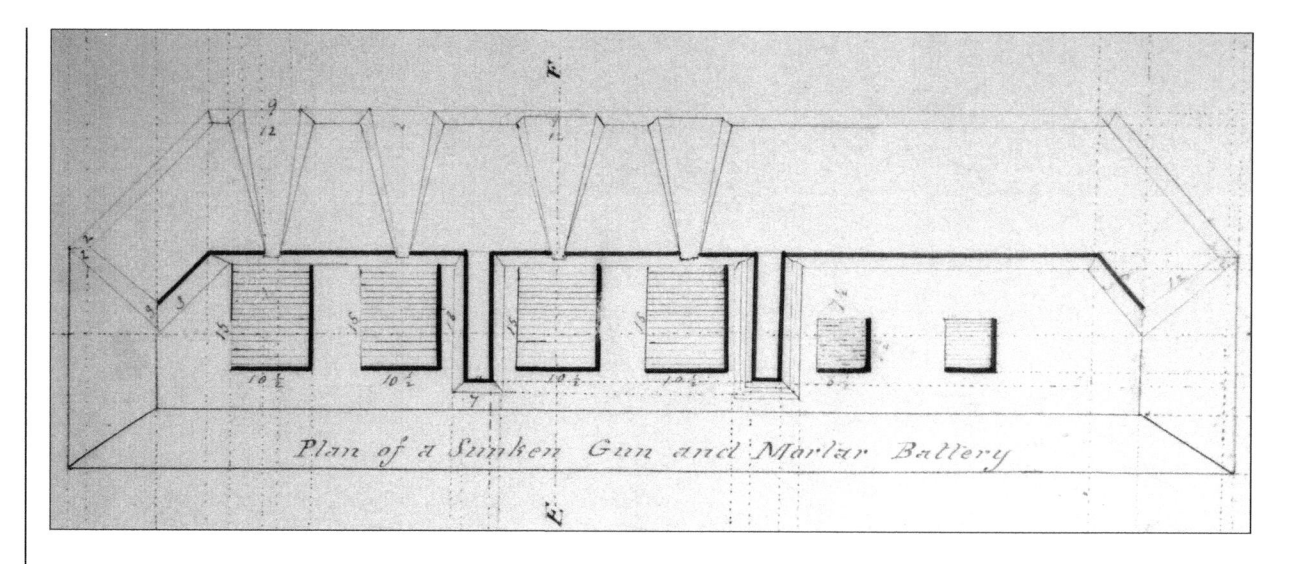

Plan of a Sunken Gun and Mortar Battery

A plan of a sunken gun and mortar battery showing the wooden platforms and the embrasures. The image is a 19th-century drawing by a gentleman cadet of the Royal Engineers which was intended to show various field engineering works to be constructed for siege batteries. This sort of work was used throughout the Napoleonic and Crimean period. (Author's Collection)

The first batteries were intended to negate enemy fire and this was ideally done by enfilading the face of the wall to be attacked. Obviously this was a complex business and a great number of different positions had to be taken up during the siege in order to achieve it since the defenses would be designed to make this process difficult. Great emphasis was placed on the concept of ricochet fire. To achieve this, a gun was placed in a position parallel to the face to be enfiladed and then its elevation was raised so that it could be fired with a reduced charge. The shot was given just enough impetus to clear the height of the other defensive walls and it would then bound along the length of the target parapet. The effect of a carefully aimed shot would be devastating, wrecking guns and equipment and killing and maiming the defenders. As a general rule the smaller the angle the shot was made to bounce, the greater would be its duration and effect. It is important to know that ricochet could be used with a howitzer shell as much as a round shot. Since it is filled with powder, one might assume it would explode on the first ricochet. The technique seems to have been the same as that used for firing shot.

The breaching guns were expected to be targeted on the crest of the glacis below the besieged fortification. It was suggested that a breaching battery be formed of four guns but this was certainly not always the case. Effecting a breach was done by a methodical battering of the wall. First the guns marked out a horizontal line about six feet from the bottom of the wall. Then they would mark vertical lines from the horizontal to the cordon on top of the revetment. Finally these lines would be continually deepened until the wall gave way. The breach was attempted about a third of the way along the the wall from the centre because that was considered to be the weakest point. It was estimated that four 24-pounders could force a breach in a reasonable thickness of wall in four to five days.

Even after the wall had given way the guns would continue to fire so that the breach would be made more accessible to an assaulting party. If normal round shot ceased to be effective, innovative practices were tried. Major Cocks described other methods used during the siege of Badajoz:

'Today some 5½ [inch] shells were thrown from 24-pounders in the hopes they would stick in the breach and have the effect of small mines. To succeed in this not only is it necessary to have long fuzes but to wad the guns, otherwise the composition melts and shells explode too soon. This being neglected, very few shells reached the breach and these did not stick in.'

Setting up a battery within range of the fortified walls was a very dangerous undertaking. Hence the need for the support of mortars and howitzers which were meant to give covering fire in order to negate the effect of enemy gunfire. Mortar batteries could continually play on the strongpoints of the defences as the effect of shell explosions inside the fortification would be devastating. Explosive shells had a way of searching the ramparts with fragments, which had a far more disruptive effect than simple round shot.

Counter-battery fire seems to have been ignored by the theorists of the day. Why this was so is difficult to fathom. In spite of this lack of written evidence it is quite clear that it was of prime importance to the practical gunner. Ensign John Mills of the Coldstream Guards, present at the siege of Burgos in 1812, related one example of how effective it could be:

'At twelve o'clock our batteries made another attempt but they no sooner opened than twelve guns were brought to bear on our three. In half an hour the battery was knocked to pieces and the men driven from the guns.'

Siege guns were normally mounted on wooden platforms and placed behind earth ramparts or gabions (large baskets filled with earth). Alternatively fascines could be used for building a gun battery. These were bundles of logs or twigs tied together to form cylindrical faggots of 18 feet or 9 feet long depending on where they were to be placed. The gabions would form the walls of the position and the fascines, covered in earth, would be used as a floor for the inner surface.

Batteries could be one of five types: cavalier, elevated, sunken, half-sunken and screen. These categories referred to the level above or below ground at which the guns were mounted. A cavalier battery was one in which the platform was above the level of the ground, a sunken battery, as its name makes clear, was excavated below the level of the ground, and a screen was a simple earth embankment thrown up to

A front and rear view of a sunken battery. (Author's Collection)

The powder magazine for siege guns could be built into their protective earthwork and this image shows a triangular magazine for such a battery. (Author's Collection)

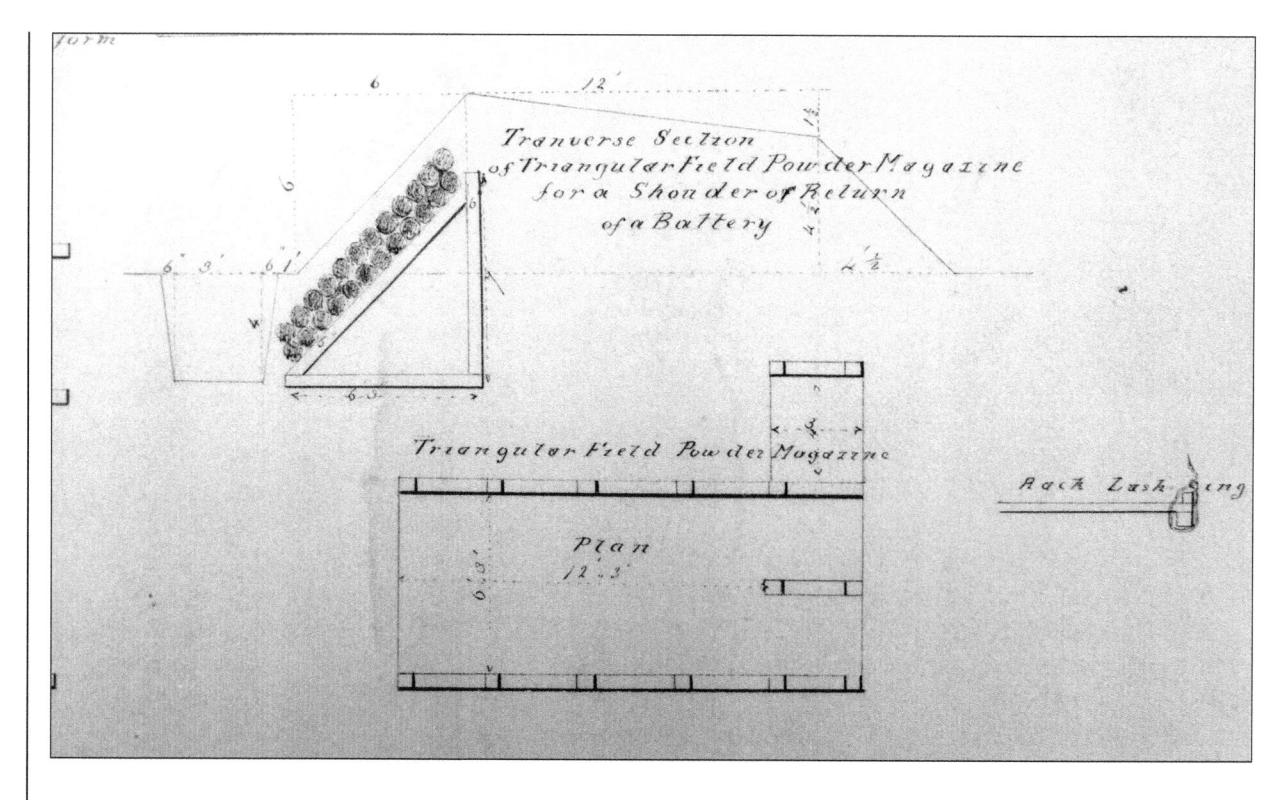

protect the guns. It was thought that a well-made earth rampart was more than capable of stopping an enemy round shot.

It was estimated that 12 workmen and eight artillerymen were needed to prepare the fascines to emplace the gun. Half the men would work in the ditch about three feet apart and dig the earth, throwing it on the berm or space between the top of the parapet and the scarp. Some of the men would work on the berm itself and the rest throw earth on the epaulment and level and compact it. The fascines were dealt with by the gunners, who calculated the length of the work and made the fascines accordingly. Twenty men could prepare a battery in 36 hours assuming each man moved 216 cubic feet of earth in the ditch in a 24-hour period.

Various tools were used to carry out this sort of work, including entrenching tools, mallets, earth rammers, saws, bills and spades. Once the area had been cleared and the earth embankment was ready, a wooden platform had to be constructed to put the guns on. These platforms were ideally based on five baulks of timber each about 6 inches square and 15 feet long. Over these were placed 14 12-inch wide planks 11 feet in length. What is not generally known is that the platform would be made with a gentle slope down towards the embrasure so that the gun would not recoil savagely off the platform. Platforms made for mortars did not need to be sloped since mortars sat on flat beds.

Once the battery was created, the guns then had to be shifted into place and invariably this required very large numbers of men and horses. One example was outlined by Sir John Jones in *Peninsular Sieges*:

'Supposing the front to be attacked to be 180 toises, with a ravelin, and the length of the first parallel to be opened the first night at 4,000 yards, it would require:

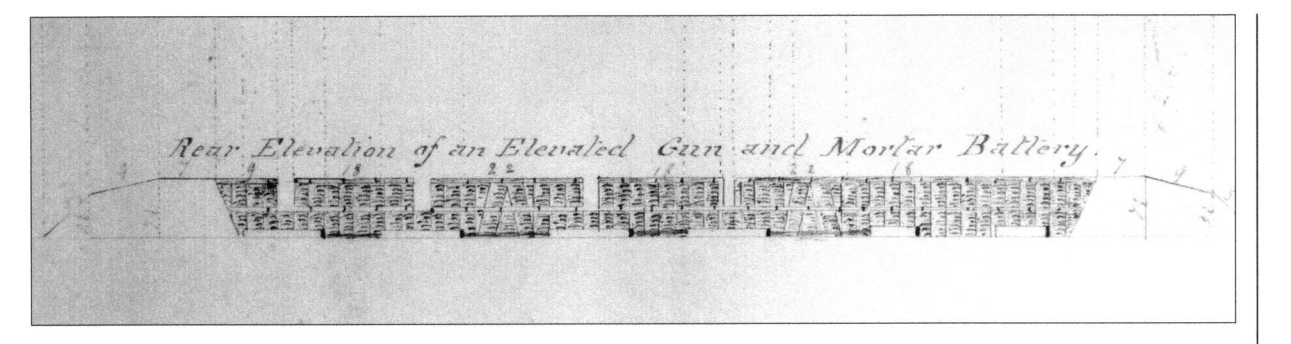

Rear Elevation of an Elevated Gun and Mortar Battery.

Plan of an elevated gun and mortar battery but with a view of the rear of the position. The artist has drawn the rear view so that the mortar platforms are on the right. (Author's Collection)

3,750 men to guard at three reliefs = 11,250
Working parties 2,000 at four reliefs = 8,000
A total of 19,250 without manning the guns.'

It was estimated that for the siege of Lille in 1794 the following siege train was needed:

64 x 24-pounder guns with 50 round shot per day and one round of case and grape shot per day

28 x 10-inch mortars on iron beds with 50 shells per day

8 x 8-inch howitzers on travelling carriages with 30 shells per day and 5 rounds of case shot per day plus 1 carcass per day

20 x 5½-inch mortars on wooden beds with 50 shells per day

All of these weapons naturally required a supply of flannel cartridges, tin tubes for ignition, portfires, fuses and match and numerous other minor items. In addition it was thought that seven spare carriages were required for the 24-pounders, two devil carriages, six sling carts, six block carriages, three forge carts, three store wagons, three triangle gyns, six laboratory tents (a tent where shells are filled and fused), two small petards and four grates for heating shot.

Powder storage was a particularly serious problem. A complex system of powder supply was normally arranged so that there was never too much in the battery magazine. Cocks described the effect of a magazine exploding:

> 'One of our magazines exploded this morning at half past 8am; it was situated in the ditch of Picurina, resting against the scarp, a live shell fell into the ditch, rebounded from the counter scarp on the magazine and instantly exploded. Ten or 12 men were hurt including four English gunners killed and about 2,000lbs of powder lost.'

Perhaps one of the more interesting examples of coastal defence in action concerned the Marcouf islands four miles off the French coast in the Bay of Normandy. In 1795 the British decided to garrison the two islands and troops were duly stationed there and blockhouses and stone gun emplacements built. By 1798 this had proved to be such an irritation to the blockaded French that they decided to try to wrest the islands back from British control. By this time there were 20 gunners and 169 Royal Marines in the garrison plus 157 other troops. Their guns were a mixed bag including 68-pounder carronades, 24-pounders, 32-pounders and an assortment of smaller calibres, all totalling 26 guns spread between the two islands. On 7 May a French flotilla of gun boats and troop transports attempted to land on the island. The gun boats may have been prames, which were specially designed flat-bottomed boats armed with 24-pounder guns. The fire of the defenders was extremely effective and managed to sink or severely damage the troop transports so that none of them was able to effect a landing. It is said that the fire of the carronades was particularly damaging, thus demonstrating an early use of the weapon in a land role.

BIBLIOGRAPHY

Both of the books produced in this series have relied on a number of primary and secondary sources. In particular readers should be drawn to the following list if they wish to study the subject further:

McConnell, D., *British Smooth Bore Artillery: A Technological Study*,
   Canadian Government Publishing Centre, 1988.

A superb study of British artillery by a Canadian expert who has looked extensively at the collections of the Royal Artillery and the Canadian Parks service. It does not cover the collections of the Royal Armouries or some of the other collections held in Britain such as the National Army Museum or the National Maritime Museum but nevertheless it is still the finest study of the subject yet produced.

Adye, R.W., *The Bombardier and Pocket Gunner*, 1802.

The original handbook for artillerists produced in 1802 and reproduced in 1813 with amendments. The Pocket Gunner was filled with information concerning gun ranges, powder charges, tactics and fortifications.

Rudyerd, C.W., *The Course of Artillery*, 1793.

A notebook produced by Rudyerd during his time at Woolwich as a cadet and including many fine drawings and sketches.

The Library of Firepower in the Museum of the Royal Artillery at Woolwich contains many notebooks on the subject of artillery, too many to mention here. They are some of the finest records of the history of artillery anywhere. In particular the notebooks written in 1793–1830 contain hundreds of fine drawings of all aspects of artillery work which have been particularly useful for the preparation of

An illustration of a siege gun and limber drawn by a cadet at the Royal Military Academy at Woolwich. The style is simplified and lacks the detail normally associated with cadets. (Courtesy RAHT)

this book. I would like to thank the Curator, Lieutenant-Colonel W. Townend, for permission to publish some of these items.

GLOSSARY

Battery In the case of siege artillery a prepared position which the guns can fire from. This would normally include a protective earthwork enclosing a wooden platform to put the guns on.

Bastion Part of a fortification extending from the main work, at the corner of two walls for example. A bastion normally had two sides and two flanks and was designed to allow flanking fire to play on an attacker trying to assault the main wall.

Cascable The portion of a piece of ordnance at the rear of the base ring.

Chase The section of a gun barrel between the second reinforce ring and the muzzle astragal and fillets.

Epaulment A parapet built on the flank of a gun battery to protect the guns and gunners from enemy fire. It can also mean an area of ground or defence that protects a gun.

Enfilade, to To fire at a unit or fortification along its length.

Embrasure An opening cut in the parapet of a fortification, through which artillery fires.

Garnish bolt One of the bolts which holds the garnish plate to the woodwork of the gun carriage.

Parapet The exterior side of the rampart that protects a defensive work.

Parallel Parallels were deep trenches dug across the face of the work to be attacked so that enemy fire could not hamper those who were working in them. Saps were normally advanced from parallels.

Rampart The raised section of the walls or embankment from which defenders fire their guns.

Ravelin A part of a fortification placed outside the main ditch having two faces forming a salient angle.

Sap A trench dug towards the defences being attacked.

Stool bed A wooden support normally positioned under the rear of the breech of the gun.

Trucks Small wheels of wood and iron fixed to a garrison carriage.

Front elevation of an elevated gun and mortar battery showing four gun positions. The mortars did not need embrasures since they fired at high angle. (Author's Collection)

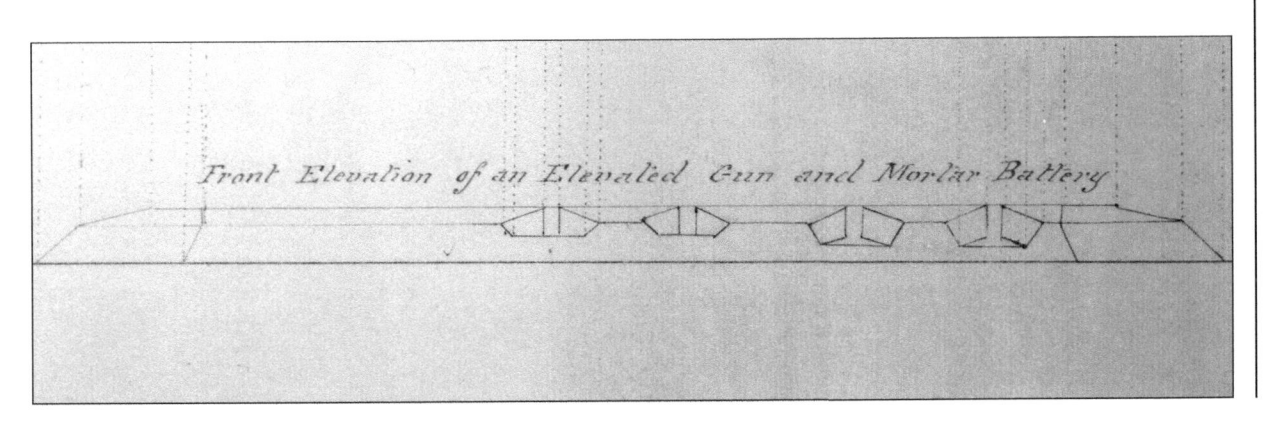

COLOUR PLATE COMMENTARY

Loading a large siege gun. This contemporary print after W.H. Pyne shows Royal Artillery gunners loading a gun. The figure on the extreme left is lighting the linstock while what appears to be the officer is handing a fixed round to the loader. The man second from right is serving the vent while the gun is being sponged to stop any embers coming up the vent. This image appears to have been executed with some knowledge of artillery drill. Note the drag rope and handspike on the ground. (Author's Collection)

A: A SELECTION OF SIEGE ARTILLERY FROM THE EARLY 19TH CENTURY

The 18-pounder siege gun is mounted on a double bracket trail carriage such as that used in the early 18th century. By the Napoleonic Wars the brackets had become elongated with many fewer garnish bolts and brackets. This image demonstrates the simple construction of the gun carriage with two main transverse bolts near the stool bed. The block trail carriage was not introduced for heavier guns, even though designs were available, until the mid-19th century, presumably because the mobility that was conferred by the block trail was not needed for a gun of position.

The 13-inch land service mortar illustrated underneath the gun has the standard type of mounting that existed from the middle of the 18th century until the middle of the 19th. It appears to have been constructed of two blocks of wood, upper and lower, fixed by bolts. In the lower bed there were four projecting lugs called traversing bolts, two on each side. These were used to lever the bed forward or backward by handspikes.

The other two images are Coehorn mortars and show the way that they could be grouped together to be fired during a siege. The gunner is igniting each mortar with a portfire. The combined explosions of ten or 15 mortar shells over a target would be a serious hindrance to the besieged troops. The inset is also a Coehorn showing a variant on the manner of securing it to the bed. Several mortars exist in the Royal Artillery and the Royal Armouries collections that have their chase bound to the front of the bed by rope tied to a metal ring sunk into the top surface of the bed.

B: PART OF A BATTERY AT THE SIEGE OF BADAJOZ IN 1811

This scene shows a battery position with two 24-pounder guns and two 8-inch howitzers of which one is shown here. According to Major Cocks, who was present at the second siege in May and June 1811, a battery was erected in front of the first parallel which held 14 24-pounders, two 10-inch howitzers and four 8-inch howitzers. The 10-inch howitzers were dismounted from their carriages and mounted on mortar frames (beds probably). The artillerymen were a mixture of Portuguese and English gunners and it is said that the ammunition was of British, Portuguese and Spanish calibres, much of which did not fit the guns properly, making much of their fire ineffective. The heavy 24-pounders were used as breaching guns and the howitzers were seemingly formed into flanking batteries to neutralise guns firing from the defences. However, it is not clear why heavy guns and howitzers were grouped together as they undoubtedly were during this siege. The illustration shows the gun carriages unpainted but they could as easily have been painted a dark grey colour as in Plate A. The small ammunition wagon at the front of the image is a copy from a contemporary illustration of a gun position during the same campaign.

C: DIFFERENT NATURES OF SIEGE ORDNANCE
1. 10-inch sea service mortar as drawn in Rudyerd's notebook of the 1790s. Compared with the land service mortar scaled next to it, the 10-inch mortar was a large weapon. Their weights were 32cwt and 4cwt.
2. 8-inch land service mortar from the 1790s.
3. 5½-inch or royal mortar.
4. Coehorn mortar.
5. Side view of a land service mortar, Coehorn.
6. 10-inch siege howitzer.
7. Frederick/Armstrong pattern gun. This was the precursor to the Blomefield gun shown below and has something of a chequered history. The design has been attributed to John Armstrong though it was certainly subsequently refined by the Surveyor of the Ordnance, Charles Frederick, in 1760 hence the double name. It was not well designed because it was so heavy and although many such guns remain in existence today they went out of service relatively quickly.
8. Blomefield pattern iron gun. Probably the most commonly seen gun on historic sites these days, the Blomefield gun was a very good design combining manageable recoil with accuracy. The loop at the back of the gun was for a breaching rope, although this was probably not used in most garrison batteries.

D: SEA SERVICE MORTARS
The sea service mortar can be seen as a siege weapon since it was primarily used to bombard coastal towns. This illustration shows the mortars in a bomb vessel as one would have appeared in the 1790s. It is thought that bomb vessels were a French invention first appearing at the end of the 17th century. The standard calibre for their mortars was 13 inches, but 10-inch mortars were common. The mortars were mounted on a centre pintle bed that could be traversed through 360 degrees. Iron and bronze mortars were used during the period. The sturdy timbers underneath each position bear witness to the enormous power of the recoil. Shot lockers were positioned under each mortar position. Mortars were initially manned by the Royal Artillery. In action bomb vessels were normally accompanied by a tender alongside that held all of the tools and equipment needed.

A typical bomb vessel with two 10-inch mortars would be supplied with 24 carcasses for each mortar, 24 common shell and 106 flannel cartridges of 5lb each. The tender would hold a further 152 round carcasses, 352 empty shells, and 4,000lb of iron shot, as well as 150 half barrels of powder. Special barrels of bursting powder were also held on the tender as well as all the fuses, priming tubes, portfires and quick match.

E: THE CARRONADE IN COASTAL USE
Although its range was limited the carronade was seen as a cheap, powerful substitute for the full-length gun when the coastal defence of Britain was considered. The mounting depicted here is somewhat conjectural because no drawings of a weapon of this type fitted on a top pivot mounting have ever been discovered. Nevertheless, carronades are frequently recorded as being the armament of Martello Towers, even though an 18-pounder gun was normally mounted atop such fortifications. However, a type of carriage known as the 'ingenious device' was designed for mounting carronades in a Martello Tower. The upper drawing shows a carronade as the main armament in a tower in this way. Although carronades were normally considered as secondary armament it is possible that they were mounted as main armament and hence this image is a possible solution. It is thought that they were mounted on centre pivot mounts in Canada but defences there were different in design to those intended for Britain. Drawings exist for iron howitzers to be used on a centre pivot mounting and the lower drawing in this reproduction is a suggestion that carronades were also mounted in a similar way, but we have no definite way of knowing. A block trail carriage was also designed for the carronade but may have come into service after the Wars.

A Coehorn mortar on a wooden bed. (Courtesy of the Trustees of the Royal Armouries)

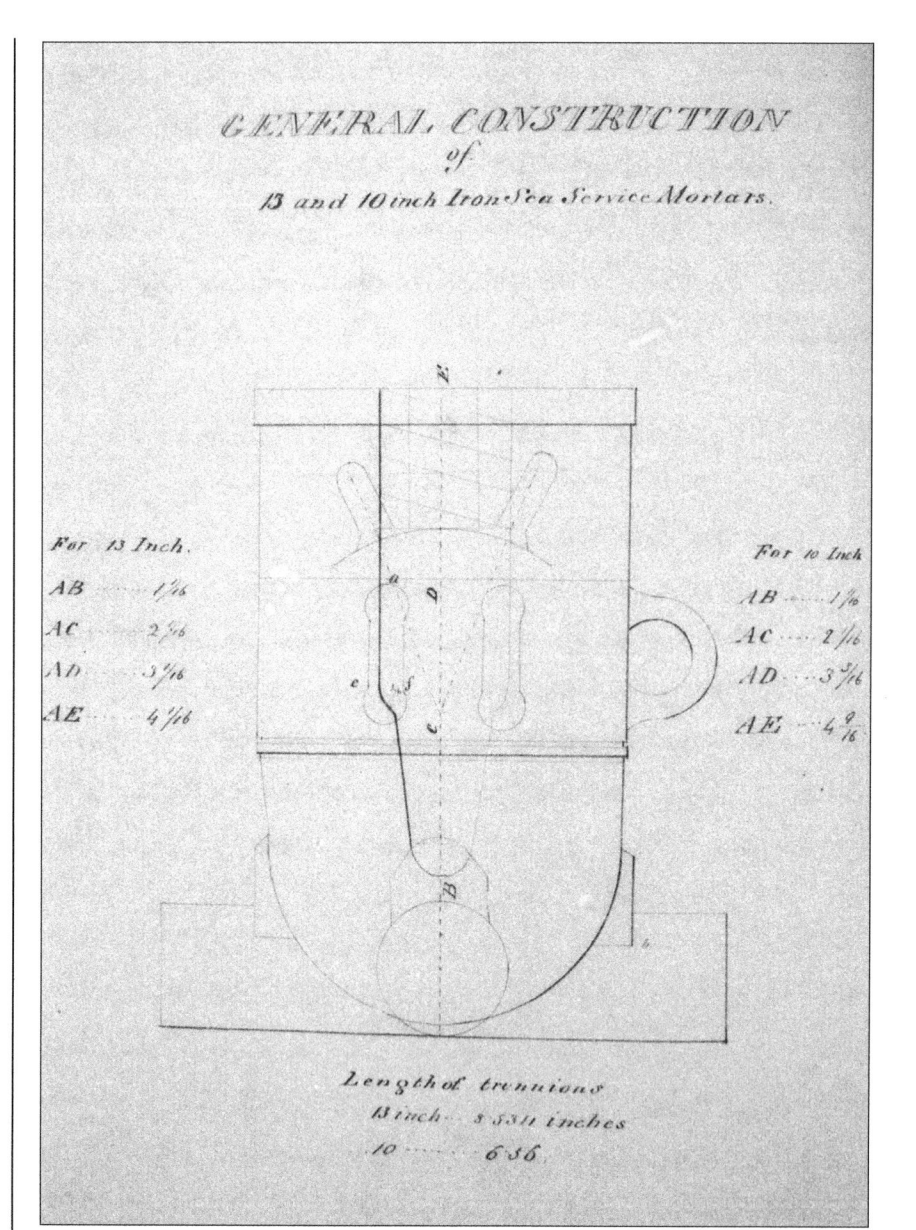

RIGHT An 18-pounder Blomefield gun on a garrison carriage. This is a typical coast defence weapon of the period 1793–1815. Very few guns are illustrated with a breaching rope in place as would usually be the case with naval weapons. It is therefore fair to assume that this type of tackle was not used in garrison service. (Courtesy of the Trustees of the Royal Armouries)

General construction of 13-inch and 10-inch iron sea service mortar. This contemporary drawing shows the longer barrel needed for sea service weapons. (Courtesy RAHT)

F: COASTAL DEFENCE GUNS IN A BATTERY POSITION

Two Blomefield iron guns are shown in this position. The left hand gun is mounted on an iron carriage of a type which is thought to have been patented by Stephen Remnant, Master Smith to the Board of Ordnance, in 1761. This consisted of two cast iron frame cheeks fitted over iron axletrees with the same kind of iron trucks as the common standing carriage. The carriages themselves resisted the weather but not enemy fire and when struck by round shot shattered into deadly fragments. They were eventually withdrawn from service. The other carriage is a common standing carriage of wood mounting an 18-pounder Blomefield gun. The garrison carriage was very similar to the naval version but had iron trucks. Each of the guns is fitted with a firing lock and lanyard. The firing lock did not catch on as quickly in the army as it did in the navy. The Admiralty had certainly looked at gun locks as early as 1755 but they did not come into general use until Sir Charles Douglas introduced them for his own ship between 1778 and 1782. The navy adopted them in 1790. The lock itself was fitted to the vent field of the gun by two bolts passed through the lock and into the pre-drilled vent field and secured by two nuts on the other side of the vent field. Since the iron guns used for garrison work were often naval pattern guns it is likely that these locks were fitted onto some garrison guns from an early date.

G: TWO EXAMPLES OF COASTAL DEFENCE WEAPONS

The upper drawing is a centre pivot traversing mount consisting of an upper common standing carriage on a lower carriage. The centre pivot and race enabled the gun to be moved in a very wide arc. The trucks were constrained on runners on the lower carriage to guide them on recoil. The blocks and tackles at the rear have not been attached so that the gun can be run out. It is not certain whether there were platforms provided at the side of the guns for the gunners to work the gun as later developments suggest. The addition of these platforms does not appear in any image until later in the century suggesting that they were not used during this period. If this is the case then it must have been an extremely difficult job to load, aim and fire the gun. It is likely therefore that some form of platform was in existence to help the gunners load and lay the gun but as yet no source has been found to confirm exactly how this was done. By the 1850s traversing carriages had side platforms and this was probably the case during the early 1800s.

The lower image shows the design for depression firing based on that initially developed by Lieutenant Khoeler during the siege of Gibraltar in the 1780s. This is a slightly later version and is shown with a pivoting stool bed. Even as late as the 1840s this type of carriage was still in use by the Royal Artillery. The 1780s design was different in that the bed was raised or lowered and pegged in position on a frame at the rear of the gun whereas this version uses an elevating spindle, which allows the gun to be depressed to an angle of up to 30 degrees.

A 68-pounder iron carronade mounted on a garrison truck carriage. The 68-pounder was the heaviest of all the carronades manufactured. They are mentioned as flanking defence or secondary armament for coastal defence. (Courtesy of the Trustees of the Royal Armouries)

INDEX

Figures in **bold** refer to illustrations

Adye, R.W. 13, 23
Almeida 3
American Independence, War of 8
ammunition 20–22, 38, 39, 41, **D**
Armstrong, John
    gun designs 5, **C**

Bacon, Anthony 7
Badajoz, siege of (1811) 5, 11, 36, 38–39, **B**
batteries 37–40, **37**, **38**, **39**, **41**, **43**, **B**
Beresford gate 11
Blomefield, Thomas
    gun designs 5, 6, **6**, 7, 9, **10**, 11, **34**, **35**, **47**, **C**, **F**
Bowen, William 12
breaching 38–39
Buenos Aires 36
Burgos, siege of 39

carriages **5**, **6**, **9**, 14, 15–18, **16**, 19–20, **20**, **23**, **35**, **36**, **47**, **A**, **B**, **F**
Carron Iron Works 6, 8
carronades 6, 7, 8, **9**, 34, 41, 42, **47**, **E**
ciphers
    George III **15**
    Townshend, George, Viscount **10**
Ciudad Rodrigo, siege of (1812) 16
coastal defences 3, 4–5, 8, 34–36, 41–42, **47**, **E**, **F**, **G**
Cocks, Major E.C. 11, 34, 37, 38–39, 41
Coehorn mortars 13, **45**, **A**, **C**
Congreve, William 15
    carriage designs 15, 18
Cooks, John, Lieutenant 15–16

Dickson, Sir Alexander, Major-General 36, 37
draught animals 18, 33

1812, War of 15
earthworks **24**, 39–40, **39**
embrasures **19**, **38**
emplacement **17**, 34–35
equipment 22–23, 39, 40, 41, **G**
Erebus, HMS 15

fascines 39, 40
Frederick, Charles
    gun designs 5–6, **C**

Fuentes d'Onoro, battle of (1811) 3

Gascoigne, Charles 8
Gibraltar 33
    siege of (1781–83) 3, 33–34, **G**
Gibreauval 35
Gomer chambers 13
guns **3**, **4**, 4, **42**, **A**, **B**, **C**, **D**
    bronze 5, 6–7, 10–12, **10**, **11**, 13, 14, 34, **35**, **36**, 37
    design 5–6, 7–9
    dimensions 8–9, 13
    iron 5–7, 11, 12–13, **14**, 14, 34, **34**, **35**, **37**, **46**, **47**
    loading 44
    mobility 4–5, **5**
    production 6–7, **8**
    repairs 36–37
    sight scales **10**
    testing 9–10
    transporting 18–20
    see also carronades; howitzers; mortars
gyns 19, **21**

Henckell and Company 6
howitzers 10, **11**, 11, 14, 17–18, 34, 38, 39, **B**, **C**

Ireland 34
Jones, Sir John
    Peninsular Sieges 40–41

King, John and Henry
    gun designs **11**, **35**

Lille, siege of 41
Low Moor Iron Company 6

Marcouf islands 41
Martello Towers 8, **E**
McHenry, Fort 15
McLeod, General 36
Melville, General 8
Mercer, Cavalié 23
Mills, John, Ensign 39
mortars 10, **10**, 11–14, **12**, **14**, **15**, 18, **22**, 34, **34**, 39, 40, **45**, **A**, **C**
    sea service 13, **46**, **C**, **D**
    shells 13
mountings **3**, **10**, **11**, 11, 12, **15**, 16–17, **34**, **35**, **45**, **A**, **E**, **G**

naval armaments 4–5, 8, 10, 12, **47**

Ordnance, Board of 6, 7, 17

Peninsular War (1808–14) 4, 10, 18, 33, 36
personnel 23–24, 41
petards 14
powder storage **40**, 41

Remnant, Stephen
    carriage designs **35**, **F**
ricochet fire 38
rockets 15
Royal Artillery 3, 12, 23, **44**
Royal Artillery Library 17
Royal Engineers 37
Royal Irish Artillery 36
Royal Marine Artillery 12
Royal Military Academy 23, **33**
Royal Military Repository 19
Royal mortars 13
Royal Navy 8
Rudyerd, C.W.
    Course Artillery 11, **C**

saps 37
shells 10, **13**, 20, 38, 39
shot 21–22, 38, 39
Shrapnel, Henry 22
sling carts 19
sling wagons 19–20, **22**
Spain 5, 33
spherical case 20, 22
stone mortars 13–14

training 18–19, 23–24
transport 18–20
traversing platforms 3, **18**
trenches 37
trucks **20**
trunnions **7**, 9, **23**

unbushing 36–37

Valetta, siege of (1800) 36
Verbruggen, Jan 12

Wellington, Duke of 33, 36
West Indies 24, 35–36
Williams, Colonel 3

Printed and bound by CPI Group (UK) Ltd, Croydon, CR0 4YY
01/07/2022
03133110-0005